The Host in the Machine

CHANDOS
INTERNET SERIES

Chandos' new series of books are aimed at all those individuals interested in the internet. They have been specially commissioned to provide the reader with an authoritative view of current thinking. If you would like a full listing of current and forthcoming titles, please visit our website www.chandospublishing.com or e-mail info@chandospublishing.com or telephone number +44 (0) 1223 499140.

New authors: we are always pleased to receive ideas for new titles; if you would like to write a book for Chandos, please contact Dr Glyn Jones on e-mail gjones@chandospublishing.com or telephone number +44 (0) 1993 848726.

Bulk orders: some organisations buy a number of copies of our books. If you are interested in doing this, we would be pleased to discuss a discount. Please e-mail info@chandospublishing.com or telephone number +44 (0) 1223 499140.

The Host in the Machine

Examining the digital in the social

ANGELA THOMAS-JONES

CHANDOS
PUBLISHING

Oxford Cambridge New Delhi

Chandos Publishing
Hexagon House
Avenue 4
Station Lane
Witney
Oxford OX28 4BN
UK
Tel: +44 (0) 1993 848726
Email: info@chandospublishing.com
www.chandospublishing.com

Chandos Publishing is an imprint of Woodhead Publishing Limited

Woodhead Publishing Limited
80 High Street
Sawston
Cambridge CB22 3HJ
UK
Tel: +44 (0) 1223 499140
Fax: +44 (0) 1223 832819
www.woodheadpublishing.com

First published in 2010

ISBN:
978 1 84334 588 6

British Library Cataloguing-in-Publication Data.
A catalogue record for this book is available from the British Library.

Typeset by Domex e-Data Pvt. Ltd.
Printed in the UK and USA.

Printed in the UK by 4edge Limited - www.4edge.co.uk

Contents

About the author

Angela Thomas-Jones is a part-time academic at Murdoch University, Western Australia, and editor of the Popular Culture Collective's community and hub projects. Angela's research pieces focus on different aspects of popular culture such as fashion, body politics, the Internet, creative industries and youth.

She can be contacted on *A.Jones@murdoch.edu.au*

Introduction

I always thought that when I received an invitation to my high school reunion I would feel nervous about attending. I thought that I would be filled with feelings of anxiety regarding what everyone would think about me. Would they recognise me? How would I summarise what I have been doing for the past ten years? When the invitation to my reunion eventually came, it was from my school friend who posted to my *Facebook* wall. She wrote, 'Hey AJ – I created an event from you and me for Dec 20th (Sat night) to catch up for a few drinks and celebrate being free from MSHS for 10 years … Hope you don't mind?' She (We) created a *Facebook* event for the reunion and invited as many *Facebook* people from our graduating year as possible, and encouraged everyone on there to invite those we had missed. As one of the 'hosts' for the event I did my share of emailing; one group message. On the event page I could see those who were attending, not attending and the 'maybes'. I knew who was going to be there. Was I nervous? No, not particularly, and I could not really understand why.

The evening arrived and I admit I had a few butterflies, but it was more to do with not falling over in my extraordinarily high heels than seeing these ex-school friends. When I reached the venue my heart was racing as I began to wonder if anyone would actually turn up. No real invites were sent. No one had physically met to organise the event. My friend (who nominated me as a co-host) and I did not even have each other's mobile phone numbers. Finally I plucked up courage and walked through to the reserved room at the back of the bar. There stood 50 people – half of our school year – mingling.

I would like to say that this story ends here and that our technologically savvy way of organising a school reunion was a success, but truth be told the evening was slightly odd. Those who were 'invited' second hand (not through *Facebook*) were irritated and vocal about the event being a '*Facebook*' reunion. The remaining people who were members of

Facebook either knew everything about what I had been doing from my profile or were irritated that I had not added them as a friend. I overheard someone asking 'haven't you read my profile?' I also found myself proclaiming that I had not been on *Facebook* in a few days in order to placate would-be *Facebook* friends who I did not want on my network. At the end of the night I realised why I had not been terribly nervous. This was because I knew what most of the people were going to look like and what they had been doing for (at least) the past year. I should really have been more nervous because, in essence, it was a social non-event. Years of wondering what old friends had been doing or avoiding irritating people that you hoped would not turn up had been turned on its head by an online social network.

It would appear that online social networks have infiltrated our lives either by participation or by lack thereof. Those who engage or have been engaged with these networks are not always willing, active and happy users. Navigating this terrain can be socially nourishing, but also destructive. This book is an exposé, revealing the types of social networks and how they affect a user's everyday life. Social networking can add 'social' value to a user's life, but this book shows how the negative undercurrents found in their 'everyday' use marks them as an insidious and destructive organism – a host in the Internet machine – whose lifeblood and their actions consists of the users and their communications.

The title of this book is an adaptation of Gilbert Ryle's 'the Ghost in the Machine'.[1] Ryle's dogma found in *The Concept of Mind* critiques Descartes' theory of a dualism between mind and body. Arthur's Koestler's *The Ghost in the Machine*, taken from Ryle's work, explores 'man's predicament' and predisposition for self-destruction.[2] It is not the intent of this book to apply Ryle's or Koestler's work to social networks. *The Host in the Machine* is informed by the work of Georg Simmel and Walter Benjamin. This is in terms of their works' emphasis on aspects of the 'everyday'. I use the words informed by, rather than applies, because this text is not specifically focused on theorising or questioning social networks in a typically academic manner. I am predominantly concerned with exposing the unique yet banal, and everyday, use of social networks. As an academic and social network user, I sway between being a critic and fan of, as well as showing contempt for, social networks. This is not an excuse for academic laziness, rather a comment on the extent to which these networks infiltrate my own life and the difficulty of remaining unbiased, yet critical of something that I am permanently linked to. Moving from the critical to the personal shows how everyday use has influenced my own life and demonstrates the ease with which good networking experiences can go bad. In relation to Simmel's approach to everyday modernity Ben Highmore writes:

> Simmel's refusal of the unifying system, the philosophical macroview, is not the attempt to find a form of attention that is adequate (more adequate) to its object (everyday life in the modern world). To synthesize this into a system would mean erasing not just the singularity of the detail, but the vitality of the relations between details.[3]

It is my aim to reveal the importance of the commonplace components of social networking. I definitely lean towards an explanation, rather than theorisation, of the details and use of the social network system. I provide examples of personal experiences with various social networks in order to delve in to my own modern user experience. Although social networking lends itself to cultural, psychological and philosophical criticism, this exposition is focused on the presence and actions of users within social networks and how these impact on everyday life. The following quote by Simmel lights the stage for my project:

> The fact that people look at and are jealous of one another, that they write each other letters or have lunch together, that they have sympathetic or antipathetic contacts, quite removed from any tangible interests, that one person asks another for direction and that people dress up and adorn themselves for one another – all the thousands of relations from person to person, momentary or enduring, conscious or unconscious, fleeting or momentous, from which the above examples are taken quite at random, continually bind us together. On every day, at every hour, such threads are spun, dropped, picked up again, replaced by others or woven together with them. Herein lie the interactions between atoms of society, accessible only to psychological microscopy, which support the entire tenacity and elasticity, the entire variety and uniformity of this so evident and yet so puzzling life of society.[4]

This book reveals the function, presence and level of use of social networks in order to stimulate future debate about why users need such an exhaustive level of communication within everyday life. In terms of communication and the 'screen' that exists between the user and social network, my work is also informed by Walter Benjamin's comments regarding a screen actor's performance. He suggests:

The screen actor's performance thus undergoes a series of optical tests. This is the first consequence of the state of affairs arising out of the fact that the screen actor's performance is mediated by the camera. The second consequence is that the screen actor, by not presenting his performance to the audience in person, is deprived of the possibility open to the stage actor of adapting that performance as the show goes on.[5]

I am not specifically focusing on users as performers, although a disconnected relationship exists between a 'screen' actor/user and their audience, which is mediated through a camera, or in this case screen. Social networks are focused on connecting people, but the existence of the screen can create difficulty in communication. This difficulty in communication is exacerbated by a disbelief in the acceptance of the Internet and relationships therein as 'real'. Throughout this book I link back to the idea that many people *act* as if virtual spaces exist outside the real world. It is the actions of users within social networks (as I describe here) and the language used in discussions on the subject which lead me to the belief that virtual and real worlds are still considered separated. The language that is used to discuss this subject suggests that a dualism between real and virtual still exists. Turkle's 1995 *Life on the Screen* highlighted a split between virtual reality and the real world.[6] Fourteen years later, writers continue to make distinctions between the virtual and real world.[7] This is observed in suggestions such as 'just as virtual worlds are similar to the real world in many ways, yet radically different in others, so too are virtual communities like real-world communities in some ways (e.g., hooligans and mashers inhabit both), yet radically different in others'.[8] I am not ignoring the presence of virtual worlds but rather that virtual worlds operate in the real world, not in opposition to it. I, like Jordan[9] and Jones & Ortlieb,[10] 'argue against such an ontological separation'. Offline and online environments have been drawn together and both are a part of the real world. Brigitte Jordan suggests:

> ... what we once called 'virtual' has become all too real, and what was solidly part of the real world has been overlaid with characteristics we thought of as belonging to the virtual. The very fact that these terms have become problematic allows the speculation that the underlying dualism itself is in some ways becoming less significant.[11]

I agree with Jordan's sentiments and it is for this reason that I use the terms online and offline to describe the user's relationship with the Internet and social networks. The computer screen is a doorway to the 'Internet', but the fact that the Internet is still regarded by many users in a 'what happens in Vegas, stays in Vegas' manner indicates that there is a gulf in knowledge regarding appropriate forms of communication. Like the actor, users can monitor, change and update their digital presence, but the communication is mediated by a screen and users are deprived of the ability to instantly adapt their behaviour, as they might in a face-to-face situation.

Unlike childbirth, when a user is born into the Internet there are many instruction booklets. A user can choose where, when and how they create their digital presence. A user enters into an online space filled with infinite creative possibilities, but similar to offline environments, life spent online is influenced by the culture and communities that surround them and in which they participate. The Internet might be physically intangible, but it nonetheless exists in the real world. The social network sites that exist within it do not operate in a vacuum. They function as part of a machine. Within this book I spend a significant amount of time describing the functions and structures of different networks, in order to show the similarities and differences between the networks. These structures and functions also define network patronage and enable in-depth, multilayered socialising. Detailing the inner workings of these networks shows the layers of connectivity available to, and between, users. Internet social networks act as a conduit between online and offline participation. The details that are released onto these sites combine to build a user's digital presence. This is where *The Host in the Machine* begins.

Birth

Social interaction via the Internet is undertaken in many formats. Online gaming, trading, chat forums, blogs, dating websites and social network sites are some of the main areas where users can create their digital presence and interact with others. There is a vast difference between the character that you might create in a massively multiplayer online game such as *World of Warcraft* and the user profile that is posted in *Bebo* or *MySpace*. All of these different digital interactions influence and shape a user's digital presence. Chapter two commences with a discussion of digital presence and how it is shaped by a user's participation in online social networks. The term 'digital presence', rather than 'digital or virtual self' is the focus because I believe that the digital presence is not separated from the self, but is simply a snapshot of parts of a user's life. In the later chapters of this book the significance of this overlap is considered in detail. Although it is recognised that this presence is still a performance and a snippet of a person's existence, the foundations of it are still informed by aspects of the user's life offline.

The Host in the Machine begins with a discussion of what is involved in this form of identity creation. Each social network allows a user to include as much information as they desire, but there is certain information that is necessary, such as name and date of birth. The user can choose to reveal only partial amounts of this information on their actual profile, but they have to submit a certain amount of information into the system in order to be allocated a profile on the network. Chapter two, 'Name/age/education/relationship status: creating a digital presence', discusses profile creation. This chapter looks at the criteria that a user submits to a number of popular networks including *MySpace*, *Facebook* and *Twitter*. This section commences by scrutinising the required 'About Me' information that allows a user to create an account. From here I begin to explain the types of information that are channelled through the different websites, including status updates, walls and photographs. I look at how different social networks cater to different social demographics, which leads to a discussion on how to navigate these different systems. *MySpace*, *Facebook* and *Twitter* have been chosen because of the size of their audience, the similarity in (some of) the content that is required and the different type of networking that occurs there. The existence of 'purpose'-built networking warrants a detailed discussion of choosing and navigating these networks. The differences in technology and style employed by these websites requires a technical knowledge both of the Internet and the different aspects of the user's digital presence. This chapter begins to unveil the relationship between the 'user' and their social network(s) of choice.

Chapter three looks at the digital presence in terms of the relationship between users and celebrities within social networks. This is in order to show how social value is added to a user's life through the presence of celebrities in social networks. The chapter is split into two main themes: how social networks affect celebrities and how celebrity is created through social network sites. In the context of this debate celebrity is important because the relationship between the network and the individual is so highly visible. Identity is also an important part of this discussion. Anyone can create a user profile so it is difficult to reliably identify if the user profile of a celebrity is that of the actual celebrity. This discussion begins by looking at the way that 'fake' profiles impact on a celebrity's real identity. Once a profile is recognised as that of a real celebrity, other issues can arise. Those on the precipice of celebrity seem to be the most likely to fall prey to profile attack. Due to the nature of celebrity, the relationship between celebrity, friends, social activities and privacy is of importance to this debate. This liaison between celebrity and network is an apposite example of how these systems, and the undercurrents found in their everyday use, impact on the user.

Life

The chapters in 'Life' observe the ways in which online social networks can impact on other aspects of a user's life. Chapter four explores socialising within the network. The user, profile content and type of network combine to show the importance of the 'social' in social network sites. 'Friends' are one of the most important elements of these systems and are also a focal point of this chapter. They are what create the social 'feel' of the websites, and without these the websites would be no more than a collection of résumés, photograph albums and biographies. The concept of 'friends' is also a pertinent point of discussion for this project because the way that the 'friends' systems work on these social networks differs from how offline relationships function. The relationship(s) between the user and their account, the account and friends, as well as the user and friends is of great importance in this debate. The 'real-time' aspect of this social circle, developed through chat functions and mobile access, is what allows the social network organism to live. The constant updates to status, photographs, videos and profile pictures, as well as the ability to comment and discuss these, reveal how pivotal offline aspects of the user's life are to the 'social' aspect of the site. With this in mind the type of 'information' that is disclosed and to which 'friends' also needs to be scrutinised. It is here where we begin to recognise the potential pitfalls of broadcasting 'too much' or 'controversial' information within these networks.

'(Net)Working: online social networks and the New Economy' commences with an exploration of the history and changing shape of work, the concept of work in the New Economy and the popular cultural workplace. It observes how technology has influenced the contemporary workplace and specifically looks at three areas concerning social networks in the workplace: the use of social networks for work-related purposes, socialising on networks at work and how the information disclosed in a user profile outside of work affects the user's work. Within this discussion, the way in which the digital presence encroaches on the daily offline routine is apparent. The history of a digital presence can be accessed 24 hours a day by the user or his or her friends. For example, a frivolous post uploaded at 1 a.m. on a Sunday morning and remaining unchanged until Monday may be accessed by your work 'friends' at the commencement of the week. The more information shared on these sites, the more the digital presence impacts on aspects of the user's life offline and vice versa, and although the relationships (re)formed and maintained on these networks can add value to a person's life, they can also have a negative impact. Using social networks at work is also contentious. Issues relating to the border between working using a social network and 'socialising' during work time are also discussed. This reveals the difficulties in defining digital boundaries. How a person functions outside of social networks can also influence their digital presence. My exploration of this topic, in relation to work, reveals the negative impact of everyday use on a user's life.

Death

There are many positive aspects to online social networking, especially for those who are geographically dislocated from friends and family. In recent years a sinister use of digital social networks has been observed. 'You've been poked: the relationship between social network systems, bullying and harassment' explores the nastier side of social networking. Tales of bulling and harassment have become prevalent in current affairs television, often due to the tragic conclusion of suicide. In this chapter I track some of these stories, which portray how these networks not only work as a conduit for this activity, but also provide evidence that allows the culprits to be prosecuted. I shift from the critical to the personal, with an exploration of the undercurrents that exist in online social networks. I use three personal examples to show how the everyday use of popular network functions such as status updates, photographs and chat can negatively impact on a user's life.

Social networks can add value to our lives. Technology is a part of our life and for many users social network sites are a part of life, not something separate from it. One concept that has always infuriated me is work/life balance. The reason for this is that work is not separate from life. There is an argument in anti-social network circles that too much life gets lived through these sites and not in the 'reality' of the offline world, but I would argue that these networks are as much a part of real life as emails and gossiping on the phone. They are real because they are significantly influenced by offline activities and they impact on various aspects of a user's online and offline life. These sites do not operate in a bubble and this final chapter marks the end of the digital presence life cycle. In previous chapters I recognised that there can be points when the digital presence encroaches on other parts of a user's life. The final chapter discusses the point of supersaturation and the decline of the user's interest in social networks. Addiction, affliction and boredom can come with using a network and this chapter looks at various occasions when this can occur. Much of life can be historicised in a social network and this chapter opens up the dialogue on becoming digitally dead. This discussion first looks at what happens to our digital presence when we actually die in the offline world in terms of immortalisation of the digital presence. Becoming web dead or undertaking web-suicide/webicide refers to the death or removal of the digital self from the Internet. It is also not something that is easy to do. This chapter looks at the difficulty in removing information from multiple areas of the Internet. Whether we become digitally dead or actually dead, it is difficult to remove the traces of our lives from the Internet. It is a user's choice to move on from the digital world where this discussion finds its final resting place.

Our digital presence does not dance around cyberspace without instruction; everything it does is on our command. By tracing, facing and reflecting upon the life cycle of the digital presence, this book unveils an insidiousness that is located in the everyday use of social networks. The negative undercurrents beneath the surface of a user's life challenge the idea that social networks are a predominantly positive force. They act as an entertainer, mediator and organism, and once a user engages with them (if you will excuse the dramatic reference) their relationship is not dissimilar to Borg assimilation. The level of insidiousness can only be recognized once participation has occurred, so in the words of Jean-Luc Picard, 'red alert. All hands to battle stations. Engage.'[12]

Notes

1. Ryle, G. (2009) *The Concept of Mind: 60th Anniversary Edition*. Abingdon: Routledge, p. 5.
2. Koestler, A. (1967) *The Ghost in the Machine*. London: Danube Edition, pp. xi–xii.

3. Highmore, B. (2002) *Everyday Life and Cultural Theory*. London: Routledge, p. 35.
4. Simmel, G. (1997) 'Sociology of the senses', In D. Frisby and M. Featherstone (eds) *Simmel on Culture*. London: Sage, p. 109.
5. Benjamin, W. (2008) *The Work of Art in the Age of Mechanical Reproduction*. London: Penguin Books, pp. 17–18.
6. Turkle, S. (1995) *Life on the Screen*. London: Orion.
7. See the following example articles: Nook, A.K. (2009) 'Disruption from the virtual world', *Mechanical Engineering*, 131(11): 22–9; Billings, D. (2009) 'Teaching and learning in virtual worlds', *The Journal of Continuing Education in Nursing*, 40(11): 489–91; Meyers, E.M. (2009) 'The tip of the iceberg: meaning, identity, and literacy in preteen virtual worlds', *Journal of Education for Library and Information Science*, 50(4): 226–37; Schiller, S.Z. (2009) 'Practicing learning-centered teaching: pedagogical design and assessment of a second life project, *Journal of Information Systems Education*, 20(2): 369–82; Anon. (2008) 'Terminology, contexts and distinctions', *Library Technology Reports*, 44(7): 7.
8. Anon., *op. cit.*, 7.
9. Jordan, B. (2009) 'Blurring boundaries: the "real" and the "virtual" in hybrid spaces', *Human Organization*, 68(2): 181–94.
10. Jones, R. & Ortlieb, M. (2006) 'Online place and person-making: matters of the heart and self-expression'. In: *Proceedings of the Ethnographic Praxis in Industry Conference*. Portland, OR: American Anthropological Association, pp. 197–210.
11. Jordan, *op. cit.*, p. 182.
12. Frakes, J. (1996) *Star Trek: First Contact*. USA: Paramount.

2

Name/age/education/status update: creating a digital presence

Whether it is online shopping or ranting on *Livejournal*, when a person participates in an interactive online activity they are developing their digital presence. The digital presence can be influenced by something as straightforward as *Amazon.com* automatically generating a list of 'things you might like' based on previous purchases, or it can involve the time-consuming process of developing, training and playing a character in a massively multiplayer online role playing game such as *World of Warcraft*. The way a user engages with the Internet affects their digital presence. These varied activities mean that Internet users have multiple sites of engagement, and social networks are complex nodes of this digital presence.

Accordingly, this chapter dissects the digital presence in the context of online social networks. This is in order to establish the characteristics that constitute a digital presence, and how these differ between varying social networks. These social networks have many 'tools' and requests for personal information. The amount of information a user submits can differ depending on their level of engagement, and trust, as the legitimacy of the information disclosed is uncertain. Therefore, this chapter explores how the reality of a user's life is linked to their digital presence. I begin by examining types of online networks and the information and activities required for the birth of the digital presence. By looking at gaming, online dating, blogging and social networking sites, I assert that online social networks are inextricably linked to the real world. This chapter puts forward the idea that the digital presence is never 'offline', which opens up the discussion for later chapters on how the digital presence affects the life of a user. Before this, however, the context of the digital presence needs to be considered.

I use digital presence to refer to the way that a user deploys information and activities online. Whenever a user engages with the Internet, they leave a digital trail or imprint, and as Kent argues:

> Some of these digital identities are closely aligned to an individual off screen and easily attached to an individual ... Other digital identities are more distanced and the link less strong, such as when a web page is customised based on a user's history of visits.[1]

User habits contribute to this digital identity, as our work, leisure and consumer practices impact on who we are on/offline. This aspect of digital identity is, however, not the focus of this book. The reason why I have opted to use the phrase digital presence rather than digital identity, or self, is two-fold. Identity in this book refers to the basic information that a person uses as a foundation for a user profile in an online network – such as name, age, sex and profession. Digital presence is a combination of this information and the user's online activity. Participation in this manner is not isolated from the real world and for this reason the idea of the digital self is inappropriate, as it presupposes a separation. The main focus here is on the social aspects of the digital presence. The information that people reveal as well as how they engage with, and perform in, online social networks are important elements of this examination. Although my conception of the digital presence does not focus directly on the 'self' (a subject that has been debated in relation to users' interactions with virtual environments) it does intersect these ideas.

The film *The Matrix* identifies and questions concepts of reality and ideas of the fragmented self.

> Neo: Right now we're inside a computer program?
>
> Morpheus: Is it really so hard to believe? Your clothes are different, the plugs in you arms and head are gone, your hair has changed. Your appearance now is what we call residual self-image. It is the mental projection of your digital self.[2]

In relation to cyberspace, online selves are often discussed in terms of how they differ from a user's offline self.[3] Zhao asserts:

> ... the proliferation of self in cyberspace has been explained largely in terms of the detachment of the self from the body in telecopresent inter-action: as others cannot see who we really are, we are free to claim to be whoever we want to be.[4]

This chapter (and book) is focused on presenting ideas that cut across this research. The discussion here is not focused on dissecting and deconstructing the meanings and formulations of the self. This book, working under the assumption that the self is fragmented, questions the belief that contemporary online participation exists outside of reality. This debate is centred on revealing the nature and potency of a digital presence on a user's life, at a time when the line between on- and offline is becoming blurred and demystified.

In domains of online gaming, gambling, blogging, chatting and even dating, it is easy to see how a user can reinvent themselves online. Turkle's *Life on the Screen* discussed 'how a nascent culture of simulation is affecting our ideas about mind body, self and machine'.[5] She focused her attention on multi-user domains (MUDS), looking at the creation of selves and how technology challenges offline perceptions of self. In relation to Benjamin's work regarding actors and the 'screen',[6] it is probably more appropriate to address the relationship between a user and social networks as life through the screen. The digital presence is influenced by a user's engagement with MUDS and is an example of a part of a user's life that remains online. The number of MUDS has grown dramatically since Turkle wrote her text in 1995. These different forms of MUDS needs to be contextualised within different groups of networks and approached in terms of their relationship to the idea of digital presence.

Online gaming networks are significant MUDS (although the acronym MUDS has less cultural currency than it used to) because as gaming technology evolves, player interaction and communication within the game also change. It would be problematic to suggest that the desire or requirement of a user to discard their offline self in the search of a different one is necessitated by all games. Many gamers would argue that role-playing in a game is like acting or playing 'dress-ups' and is not some latent desire to become a wizard. On some surface level the act of 'playing' in a game needs to be recognised. Role-playing is a significant part of online gaming and finds emphasis in particular Massively Multiplayer Online Role-Playing Games or MMORPGs. Story development is an important part of this. Wu, Li and Rou write:

> Like movies, most online games have a story to which players may attach their fantasies and desires. An online game story usually tells players what is going on in a game. More specifically, it describes the circumstances of the events or the experiences of the characters that happen in the game sessions [Juul 2001a]. Like those presented in movies, novels, and operas, stories are also a key component of an online game.[7]

MMORPGs are a genre of online games in which players either interact with the stories created for the game or construct/develop the story themselves. MMORPGs are pertinent examples of Turkle's idea of simulation, but they go beyond the idea of a presentation of fragmented selves, and *World of Warcraft* (*WoW*) is an exemplar.

In *WoW* gamers are expected to create their character based on one of the ten races and develop it by choosing professions and then questing. The character then adventures in a chosen realm.[8] 'As a massively multiplayer online game, World of Warcraft enables thousands of players from across the globe to come together online – undertaking grand quests and heroic exploits in a land of fantastic adventure.'[9] This game is based on questing through a fantasy world and battling creatures in a friendly social environment. Players can choose the way in which they play the game. For example, the existence of different realms allows the user to choose whether they engage in player-versus-player combat. Players are also encouraged to socialise with other players in their realm. '... the game is built to facilitate extensive in-game socialising ... You can also add players to a friends list, so you can keep track of nice and helpful players for grouping or just chatting'.[10] The difficulties of numerous adventures in *WoW* stimulate player-to-player interaction, making the game an effective social tool. Players can interact via textual chat functions and/or using audio devices. The social aspect of gameplay that is necessary to succeed means that the players are never just a character. The human behind the character is ever present.

Social interaction is an important aspect of online gameplay and in particular MMORPGs. I conducted an e-interview with long-time gaming expert Bennett Ring about online gaming, in particular MMORPGs. Ring is a games journalist and has a long history in this industry – Editor in Chief at IGN, PR Manager for Vivendi Universal Games, Deputy Editor for *PC PowerPlay* Magazine, Reviews Editor for *Atomic Magazine*. He is currently the Editorial Manager for 3 Mobile and an avid gamer. I questioned Ring about online gaming, changing technology and how these relate to communication in/outside of the game.

Angela Thomas-Jones: In the arena of online gaming what genres of games are there in the market?

Bennett Ring: Every genre these days now has an online component (aka multiplayer). The industry has realised that people are generally sociable creatures who like to play together, so being able to play with your pals is now becoming a commonplace feature. It's usually referred to as co-operative gameplay, where the human friends play together against enemy AI controlled by the game. Having said that, there are still a few genres where online multiplayer is more prevalent:

- MMORPG
- First Person Shooter
- Real Time Strategy

ATJ: What role does MMORPGs play in the realm of online gaming?

BR: It's a very specific niche, alongside your shooters, action games, etc. It's also a licence to print money for the PC gaming platform, a platform which many feel would be otherwise struggling as a gaming platform due to piracy. It's also a very tough niche to develop for, due to the scope of these titles being exponentially larger than other genres. It's much easier to create a few levels than it is an entire virtual world. However, the returns are so great when you create an MMORPG that works (see *World of Warcraft*) that there are a ton of MMORPGs in development right now. Sadly, most of them will fail miserably.

ATJ: As someone who has worked in the games industry for some time and who is also a gamer, what do you believe is the attraction of MMORPGs to gamers?

BR: Easy – it's the most all-encompassing virtual world offered by any genre. It is an early version of a voluntary *Matrix* – you leave your old life behind and step into the shoes of whoever you want to be (within the constraints of the game's universe). From 9 to 5 you flip burgers at Maccas, but from 6 p.m. until midnight you're an Elven rogue helping a group of adventurers to explore dungeons and slay dragons.

There's also the addictive element of MMORPGs. They're all about investing time to make your character level up (become more powerful/skilled), and to find bigger and better weapons and equipment. MMORPGs reward the player with shiny new things on a regular basis, to encourage repeat usage.

Finally there's the social aspect – MMORPGs are by far the most social kind of game. Where other genres limit the player to battling alongside a handful of friends, MMORPGs encourage massive groups of players to fight alongside each other – we're talking dozens of players, with newer MMORPGs supporting battles with hundreds of players. It's a great way to hang out with 30 or 40 mates ... without ever having to leave the house.

ATJ: How is technology in games allowing for greater interaction between players?

BR: Many ways. Graphical technology is closing the gap between the game world and the real – eventually you'll have a photoreal version of yourself in the game who can display facial expressions and realistic body gestures.

VOIP is still rather primitive at the moment, but as the Net's bandwidth increases and computers become more powerful, it'll be possible to have a chat system that mirrors the real world – in other words, you'll only hear those close to you, but still be able to hear bad guys around the corner. It's referred to as proximity chat, and is used in a handful of games already.

Combine these two technologies, and it'll be like you're talking directly to a precise copy of your pal. They'll be sitting at their computer, and their webcam will measure their facial expressions, mapping that to the in-game character. Their character's mouth will move exactly as they speak – it'll be like you're in the same room as each other.

I also think that video chat within games could become popular, but only for smaller groups of people (a handful at most) – you don't want to fill the entire screen with little windows of your pals.

The way in which communication takes place in MMORPGs is important to our discussion because as technology is changing, gaming communication is effectively bringing the player more and more into the game. From Ring's account of gaming we can see not only the different forms of games that are available online but also how emerging communications technology is impacting on the way games are being played. The use of photoreal technology in MMORPGs (given the number of fantasy and science fiction games) as well as strategy and first-person shooter games will add another aspect of the user's life to their gaming interactions. A significant point that Ring discussed is the reasons why people play MMORPGs. These loosely fit into the categories of escapism/fantasy fulfilment, hobby and friendship, which all fall beneath the larger banner of social interaction. Due to the multifaceted aspects of games such as *WoW*, *EVE* and *Second Life*, gamers fit into multiple categories simultaneously.

The social element of these games is based on team building, shared knowledge, collective skills and trading. Although the game might be based in a fantasy world, the communication occurring within it is between real players operating in real time. Kock states that games 'like World of Warcraft, are designed with the goal of making people forget about the real world and get immersed in multiplayer games'.[11] I disagree with Kock's sentiment. Although Ring made a similar suggestion, he also acknowledged that there are many other attractions to these games. MMORPGs exist within the real world and it does not matter how much a player pretends to be an orc or a blood elf, their interactions with other characters are still influenced by the social mores of the offline world. By this I mean that even if a player wants to create their character as a narcissistic gnome who likes to steal from people, they must be aware of the ramifications of the choice. The nature of multiplayer games (the requirement of player-to-player communication) means that some element of the offline self is always preserved online, even if this is just in the way that a player communicates. The characters in *WoW* are not just interacting with bots. The players behind the characters are communicating, trading and formulating plans of attack. In order for a player to progress in the game they have to be socially as well as technically literate, or 'if you offend fellow party members, your reputation can be affected'.[12] In this way the nature of social interaction remains largely unchanged. Although users are playing characters and the setting is fantastical, the expectations regarding communication are based in reality and are not separate from it. If I choose to unleash a tirade in a game such as this I must be ready for the consequences of that action, which might mean having to start again in another realm (server) when my party turns against me. In this way the digital presence in these social networks is presented as a character, but how this character performs is influenced by the knowledge of the player; knowledge that has been informed by real experiences both on/offline. This gameplay is similarly reflected in other MMORPGs.

EVE and *Second Life* differ from *WoW* in terms of format, but both encourage social literacy. *EVE* is a science-fiction MMORPG that is 'set 21,000 years in the future'[13] in outer space. Unlike *WoW*, players in *EVE* can only play on one server,[14] which means that they have the ability to affect everyone in the world of *EVE*.

> EVE is a single 'shard' virtual world. What that means is that everyone who joins EVE becomes a part of the same world and the same community. The industry standard for MMORPGs is to run

the game on multiple smaller servers, so called shards, so that each player only has the opportunity of interaction with a few thousand other players even if the number of subscribers can be in the millions. In EVE you have the opportunity to affect more than 250.000 other players in one way or another as all our players are a part of the same persistent universe, hosted on the world's most powerful gaming server yet.[15]

The fact that *EVE* exists on one server means that a player cannot just up and leave one server and move to another if they have a negative experience, unlike *WoW*. *EVE* also differentiates itself from *WoW* in that it does not discourage players from attacking other players. If attacks, however, are undertaken for harassment purposes only – forms of griefing – players can be banned from the game.[16] Within the context of the game, fighting is considered to be a legitimate part of player-to-player interaction.

'Griefer war decs' refers to the practice of declaring a war, typically in high-security, against a party who is not your competitor in politics, regional control, industry, or anything else, and does not want the war. Such wars are often, but not always, declared with the intent to extort money from the victim for termination of the war. While they are sometimes used for actual griefing (ie, declared only for the malicious enjoyment of seeing the victim suffer), they can also be seen as a valid playstyle, and are used by many for simple isk-making and/or combat training.[17]

Unlike *WoW*, being liked by your 'corporation' or other players is not totally necessary, but social interaction is encouraged through corporations and alliances. Each player can create their own chat groups with other players, as well as talk to people in their corporation and the solar system that they are located in. There is also the *EVE* online forum, where all facets of the game are discussed. In-game communication between players can be split between the 'friendly' player-to-player chats that are not necessarily game related and those that take place when war/battle is occurring with an opposing group. A player can be a lone pirate conducting solo missions, but be involved in non-game-related chat with other players. Or a player could join a fleet in a war against another faction and be communicating using tightly controlled, and military-based, commands via audio chat. In *EVE* both solo and group playing occurs while non-game-related social communication continues. Although *EVE* is set in a science fiction universe, the players themselves are always grounded in reality. Internet Relay Chat (IRC) and forum chat use the characters' names, but the player can switch between game- and non-game-related chat depending on which chat function they are using. Both non-game- and game-related chat is based in reality. Non-game-related communication constantly occurs between players and the game-related communication is influenced by the language and protocols of the situation. For example, corporations use a ranking system and these titles incorporate such terms as Lieutenant, Colonel, Commander, Commodore and General. During in-group role-playing mode, a corporation member is encouraged to communicate at their level. I queried Ring about these types of aspects of gameplay in MMORPGs.

ATJ: Are there rules (written and/or unwritten) that players are expected to adhere to when communicating in online games? If so does this differ from game to game and what are these rules based on?

BR: Absolutely, and yes, they differ from game to game. For example, if I'm playing a hardcore military simulator with my clan mates, we use the exact same language as used by the military. I've spent an entire day just practising virtual aircraft carrier landings with my squadron mates helping me, and a big part of that was learning the vocabulary used by the US Navy. They even created PDF files outlining all the terminology to help newcomers. As a *Top Gun* fan, knowing when to Call the Ball and actually having to do it was a major buzz!

For MMOs [MMORPGs] it really differs based on the guild you're playing in. Some are more serious, and have a chain of command and strict comm guidelines, while others love to scream and yell at each other and just have fun. However, all MMOs have their own slang used by all players, usually to define events that happen in the game world. They're also a shortened version of the word, to allow for quick typing.

For example, when somebody levels up in an MMO, they'll usually type Ding! into the chat channel, signifying the noise most games make when you level. All their pals will then type in gratz into the chat channel – as in, congratulations on levelling up mate, well done. There are literally hundreds of words associated with the biggest MMO out there, WoW.

As Ring discloses, the relationship between the player and their character as well as player-to-player communication is of great importance. For example, triumphs can be celebrated with fellow players using in-game language. In *EVE*, whether it is socialising, communicating on the forum, trading, mining or at war, the character and the player are one. The player does not switch to speaking an alien mode of language. It may be slang and grammatically incorrect, but it is still based on real words. The player uses a character to interact in the game, in whichever way that they wish. Yes, you can be a pirate, but what constitutes piracy is grounded in real ideas of piracy. This science fiction world poaches the language and systems existing in reality and applies it to a place of fantasy. Players do the same. They create and use characters and perform missions, but the way that they communicate and socialise in and around these activities is influenced by the reality of their own lives, as Simmel asserts: 'in the realm of reality every single element and event is placed in an infinitely expanding series of spatial, conceptual and dynamic relationships. For this reason every identifiable element of reality is only a fragment and not a totality.'[18] I agree and suggest that gaming, characters and avatars are all fragments of the user's reality, rather than elements that are outside of it. So the digital presence – the player's character and in-game actions – is heavily influenced by the player's on/offline life. *Second Life* is another apt example of this.

Second Life presents its game experience as something that is outside the real world.[19] This is a false dichotomy because the environment that exists in *Second Life* is informed by the 'real world'. 'The Creations' is an element of the game that allows the user the freedom to use their creative talents to bring fantasies to life. For example, a user can fly in the game, not something that you can do in the real world, but the user's talents and imagination are based outside of the game. Indeed, *Second Life* has a clear element of creativity both in terms of fantasy (e.g. giving your avatar giant wings[20] and flying around the game or living out your dream of 'being bought and used for pleasure'[21]) as well as being creative in 'real' terms such as conducting business meetings, trying out new systems or for educational purposes. *Second Life* reflects ideas of the fragmented self. For example, 50-year-old Elsinora Sideways states, 'in my real life it's difficult for me to be myself. I am a wife and a mother and there are certain expectations that come with those roles. But in Second Life, I'm free to do things that aren't appropriate for my wife and mother role. In the virtual world there simply aren't the same pressures to conform.'[22] Sideways indulges in *Second Life* to free herself from the burdens of other aspects of her life outside the game. She refers to it as a 'platform – a whole world'.[23] But it is something that is very much a part of reality. It is a game, which in one instance encourages users to live out their fantasies and on the other to practise elements of their everyday reality. So *Second Life* draws together fragments of a user's everyday reality in a multilayered environment.

Positioning a game as existing outside of reality allows users an excuse for their in-game behaviour. An avatar is created by the user and so are all of its actions. It is questionable to argue that this game operates with no effect on the real world. Mark Stephen Meadows in his exploration of *Second Life* writes:

> Most of all I found the avatar to be a machine that is attached to the psychology of its user. From within that machine the driver can peek out, squinting through alien eyes, and find a new world. And, oddly, the driver can also look into himself, as if gazing into his navel, and find a new landscape inside as well.[24]

I am not arguing that this is not a virtual world, but this virtual world is based on the real dreams and fantasies of its users. The game is just another facet of real life. What happens in the game does not stay in the game and this could be largely to do with the level of social interaction that occurs within it, in terms of both pleasure and business.

Second Life is now a significant place to conduct business. Similar to *WoW* and *EVE*, Linden dollars (the game currency) that are made in game businesses can be sold for US$ outside the game. Businesses that also exist offline are using *Second Life* for purposes such as meetings. The game's website encourages this use with 'Second Life Grid' stating:

> Second Life is the world's leading 3D virtual world environment, which enables enterprises and educators to build custom immersive spaces and applications that increase productivity, creativity, and innovation while cutting travel costs and doing business in a more eco-friendly way. Today, hundreds of global organizations, including Fortune 500 companies such as IBM and Northrop Grumman, use the Second Life to bring distributed teams together in a shared virtual workspace to collaborate, meet, learn, and prototype new offerings.[25]

Therefore, there are varying facets of *Second Life* – playing, working and learning – that allow the user to move between the different areas of their life in both on- and offline capacities.[26] For this reason it is difficult to make a separation between the player and the avatar. Like *WoW* and *EVE*, in *Second Life* the avatar/character in the game is controlled by the player and is influenced by the reality of the player's life. As suggested in the interview with Ring, these games are used as a form of release from the drudgery of other areas in a player's life. They are also a place where friendships and romantic relationships are made and maintained. Online dating is an important aspect of this debate, as it occurs both in forums and in sites that are dedicated to this form of social networking.

The relationship between dating and online social networks is two-fold. The first stream of dating relates to those who meet through an online social network and form an online relationship. The second relates to networks that are created solely for dating purposes. Obviously the two aspects of Internet dating crossover in any resulting romance but can differ in terms of intent. Online relationships are based on the interactions between people that are formed digitally but sustained both on- and offline. In order for a relationship to translate offline, the information that is disclosed online must hold some truth. The information that is divulged in the two streams of online dating differs. Online chat forums, not specifically meant for dating, do not necessarily require information about age or sex, a real name or even a biography. By contrast, online dating websites are aimed at creating a full profile so the user can attract an appropriate partner. In the first stream of dating the users develop a friendship through conversing in a forum and then offline information is disclosed privately once a rapport is established. In an online website dating situation, profiles including name, age, profession, likes/dislikes and biography are there for a user to trawl through. Once a potential friend/partner is found, communication can begin.

Online social forums whether they are chat, gaming or networks such as *MySpace* just to name a few, are spaces where like-minded users go to socialise. This socialising can then lead to dating and onward to a romantic relationship. Much has been written about the negative sides of this kind of relationship formation, namely about the abundance of paedophiles, stalkers and other fraudulent users who cruise forums. Although caution should be taken to avoid interaction with such users, the large amount of socialising that occurs online makes the Internet a prominent place to meet and form relationships. Second Lifer Elsinora Sideways was a clear example of this. She used *Second Life* as an escape from her alcoholic husband[27] and met a new one online.[28] In his poignant piece 'Love Online' Henry Jenkins recounts the reality behind his son's Internet relationship that was formed in an online discussion group:

> Sarah and Henry's romantic communication might seem, at first, more transient, bytes passing from computer to computer. Yet, he backlogged all of their chats and surprised Sarah with a printout.

In this fashion, he preserved not only the carefully crafted love letters but the process of an evolving relationship.[29]

These courtships begin as a written word, words that have been thought about, edited and posted. These are words that can be saved and that cannot be taken back once released into the world wide web. Often those relationships formed in online discussion groups are first developed in multi-user domains, and therefore the first signs of textual wooing are on show for other users to read. Jenkins goes on to write, 'Henry and Sarah would not have met outside their virtual communities the Internet facilitates. But they were both emphatic that purely digital communication could not have sustained their relationship.'[30] For a 'relationship' to be sustained the on- and offline spaces must collide. So in order for online dating to be successful the parts of the user that are projected digitally must resonate in person. There is also a clear difference between dating online and seeking out love via an online dating website.

Online dating websites are another form of online social network. The intent behind these services is to provide the user a way of forging an offline relationship.

> Most internet daters seem to regard online dating services either cautiously or light heartedly as a channel through which they may be able to find new friends as much as finding people to date. For one in five, however, there is a more serious purpose to internet dating – to find a potential mate or marriage partner.[31]

For this reason online dating has a very 'real' element. Although these dating services are offered online, the actual dating occurs offline. A prospective dater might post a photograph of their younger self or someone entirely different, but the truth will be revealed when they meet in person. This stream of online dating illustrates the problem with claiming that on- and offline lives are something separate from each other. The two environments are very much intertwined. The digital presence affects the user and vice versa. The reality of online dating or dating online is that the relationships are more than just conversing in a forum and so there are difficulties in maintaining a relationship solely in cyberspace.

Jenkins asserts the difficulty in developing a relationship online, writing 'the medium's inadequacies are, no doubt, resulting in significant shifts in the vocabulary of love. In cyberspace, there is no room for the ambiguous gestures that characterized another generation's fumbling first courtships.'[32] Jenkins' sentiments regarding the shift in the vocabulary in terms of love suggests that the Internet is challenging the way in which we communicate. Vocabulary is being modified, according to Jenkins, as participation online grows. Textual communication has to be clear, as Jenkins suggests, when dating online so misunderstandings do not occur. The subtle nuance of tone and turn of phrase have been replaced by emoticons, brackets and asterisks. Although the time constraints of gaming require textual communications to be clear but brief, dating online requires them to be clear and emotional. Although these networks require a technological literacy, they also require a social literacy, which is heavily based on acceptable behaviour in offline social interaction. The realm of online dating encourages the crossover between on- and offline environments and as technology such as VoIP (Voice over Internet Protocol) and video chat evolves it is becoming apparent that the line between the two might only be a screen. Dating online is not role-playing and whether in a game, forum or other social network the interactions between these people are not fantasy; these are people who are developing real romantic relationships with real feelings. The presence of a screen and the 'freedom' of socialising, provided through the networks' various public and private channels of communication, allow relationships to foster in a distinct manner. Although these relationships and feelings are not fantasy, the structure and style of their beginnings highlights that there is unusual impetus that informs their development. The negative side of social networks and relationship formation is something that is discussed in future chapters. The emotions felt between people are not contained in some Internet world of whimsy nor do they only exist within the forum where they were born. They are part of lives and for that reason these relationships demonstrate the blurring of the boundary between on- and offline. This highlights how the digital presence means that part of the user is always online and emphasises the importance of Internet use in everyday life.

(Web)logs are an example of a more stable online digital presence. Blogs differ from something like a personal homepage, which can often be stagnant or updated sporadically because they are like living interactive diaries.

> Routinely, blogs are defined as websites on which, dated entries are frequently uploaded and presented in reverse chronological order. Comments about any subject, of any length, can be presented to the world in this format. When, in 1999, technology had evolved sufficiently and blogs became available as hosted services (provided by Blogger, LiveJournal, and the like), their numbers rose sharply. Currently, millions of blogs can be found in cyberspace.[33]

Blogs are representative of a more stable online presence because they can be interacted with while a blogger is away from their account. Friends/followers/lurkers can read and (depending on the type of blog) comment on the blog. Blogging is far reaching, from blogging networks such as *LiveJournal*, *Blogger* and *Wordpress*, to blogs on personal webpages, news sites and many other websites, covering topics from cooking to steampunking. Many bloggers have made it their full-time occupation and some people (Perez Hilton for example) have become famous for it. MacDougall states:

> At their best, blogs represent a new form of open-sourced/open-access partisan press that promises the bring McLuhan's tribal context one step closer to fulfillment. At their worst, blogs represent the latest form of mass-mediated triviality and celebrity spectacle, with the potential to create and sustain enclaves of intolerance predicated on little more than personal illusion, rumor and politically motivated innuendo.[34]

Blogs offer a space for people to rant and rave, and for other people to engage with this. Motivation behind blogging differs from person to person, from agonising about the banalities of life to trying to start a cultural revolution. Whether gossiping, ranting, celebrating or preaching, a blog is always personal. This is the fulcrum of the digital presence. These crafted thoughts are *always* online, so effectively part of the user is always online, and as the blog evolves so does the user's digital presence. Since MacDougall's article in 2005 the prevalence of a different form of open-access network has gained extensive popularity. Social network(ing) sites incorporate blogging and other elements of a user's life and like weblogs they are entirely dependent on the user's reality.

There are a number of social networking sites that are specifically focused on socialising and these are the main focus of this book. Online social networking site *SixDegrees*.com, launched in 1997[35] has been noted as one of the earliest formations of this networking system.[36] Some noteworthy networks that followed on from *SixDegrees*.com were *BlackPlanet* (1999), *MiGente* (2000), *Cyworld* (2001), *Friendster* (2002), *LinkedIn* (2003), *MySpace* (2003), *Facebook* – Harvard Only (2004), *Flickr* (2004), *Bebo* – relaunched (2005), *Facebook* – highschool networks (2005), *Facebook* (2006) and *twitter* (2006).[37] Boyd and Ellison argue:

> What makes social network sites unique is not that they allow individuals to meet strangers, but rather that they enable users to articulate and make visible their social networks ... On many of the large SNSs, participants are not necessarily 'networking' or looking to meet new people; instead, they are primarily communicating with people who are already a part of their extended social network. To emphasize this articulated social network as a critical organizing feature of these sites, we label them 'social network sites'.[38]

While I agree with boyd and Ellison that a large amount of interaction in these networks is between friends or acquaintances, categorising this as their only function is ignoring the breadth of their usage – *twitter*, for example, challenges this assumption. These networks are used for interacting with friends and acquaintants, business networking and making new friends, all by relaying different forms of information. Boyd and Ellison argue that:

> While we use the term 'social network site' to describe this phenomenon, the term 'social networking sites' also appears in public discourse, and the two terms are often used interchangeably. We chose not to employ the term 'networking' for two reasons: emphasis and scope. 'Networking' emphasizes relationship initiation, often between strangers. While networking is possible on these sites, it is not the primary practice on many of them, nor is it what differentiates them from other forms of computer-mediated communication (CMC).[39]

I disagree with their claim, as the networks that they focus on are used in varying capacities. As Beer suggests, 'why not stick with the vernacular terminology, social network- ing site, which is more differentiated and descriptive of the processes, rather than moving toward this re-definition forwarded in boyd and Ellison's article?'[40] In this and subsequent chapters the terms social network and social networking are used interchangeably because the websites that this book focuses on (*MySpace*, *Facebook* and *twitter*) are online social networks where social networking occurs.

It is difficult to pinpoint the exact audiences that each online social network is aimed at, but the digital presence does demonstrate the way that a user can engage with different networks. There is some commonality between social networks as a certain amount of information must be disclosed in order to set up profiles. 'The profile is generated using the answers to these questions, which typically include descriptors such as age, location, interests, and an "about me" section. Most sites also encourage users to upload a profile photo.'[41] The 'About Me' information is where the digital presence is born. It creates the 'identity' for the digital presence. Lahlou asserts that 'there are several ways of defining identity: physical (subject as a body); social (subject as a social position); biographical (subject as the product of past experiences and desires'.[42] Biographical information constitutes 'identity' in the context of the digital presence and this text. There is the potential for people to create fraudulent profiles and there is much written on the subject of privacy issues concerning the disclosure of personal information within social networks. Although this is a pertinent topic for criticism it falls outside of the scope of this book. The majority of profiles created within social networks contain a certain amount of real information, as the user's actual friends often view them. This disclosure of 'About Me' information plays one part in the birth of the digital presence. It is also evidence of how the digital presence and engagement in social networks is grounded in the real world of the user. Depending on the social network, the user can decide what kind of information is revealed – this might range from a name only, to every minute detail of their life; from birth, though school, to employment history. Types of other functions available on these networks – music, games, chat, video, photographs – contribute to user interactions within the network, which in turn helps identify patronage. So while an audience is not defined by age, race, culture or social status, it can loosely be organised by the website's different functions.

MySpace was certainly not the first online social network, but it was probably the first to garner a substantial amount of attention. This network has received both positive and negative attention. It has been tagged as a springboard for such musical acts as The Arctic Monkeys and Lily Allen, a place for unsigned musicians to be heard, a haven for music fans and a home to a number of net-celebrities. *MySpace* has also been linked to the emo culture, multiple suicides and a place for bullying to occur. The *MySpace* website offers the user the ability to create a profile that contains the 'About Me' style of information. It also allows the user to present a unique layout, upload a profile picture, blurb, comment, video, blog, instant messaging and webmail. The website itself also contains other pages that users/non-users can interact with – music, video and celebrity updates. Probably the most important are the music pages. *MySpace* contains the profiles of thousands of signed and unsigned musicians. These pages contain information about the act as well as videos, blogs and MP3s. Some songs are available to download free, and others can be purchased through the site or have links to the *iTunes* store. *MySpace* also has regional websites. The user can sign in to their country's network, which highlights local music acts. This selection alters such information as the 'Featured Artists' on the music page. *MySpace* is very focused on the engagement with music and the world of musicians. 'Today on MySpace' features the latest music, music videos and celebrity updates from musicians.[43] In their profiles users are encouraged to reveal information about their favourite popular cultural texts – music, books, films, heroes – and can also become 'friends' with their favourite bands and other popular cultural figures such as actors and characters. The profile content and focus on music pages in *MySpace* fosters an audience who are looking to network with friends and potential friends, fans and artists, in a system that connects with and shows their preferences in popular culture. The user's digital presence evolves when they change their mood, update their blurb and blog about their life. 'Friends' have the opportunity to comment on these remarks. The blurb, photographs and blog show the user's *MySpace* history and expand the user's digital presence. These features, if left unchanged, are always available and never go 'offline'. This presence can have a significant impact on other aspects of the user's life, which is discussed in later chapters. *Facebook* influences a user's digital presence in a similar manner, but it promotes a different type of social networking.

Facebook, like *MySpace*, requires the 'About Me' style content and, again, how much of this information is revealed in a profile is up to the user. *Facebook* provides the user space to expand their profile by uploading albums of photographs, videos and links. Similar to *MySpace*, *Facebook* also has a webmail chat function. A user also has a 'boxes' page on their profile that can be filled with the results from any *Facebook* applications that they have engaged with. The application function on *Facebook* is unique to the network because these range from quizzes, such as 'Which 1950's Pin-Up Girl are you?' to sending gifts and games. The game applications within *Facebook* operate as mini social networks, where a user can interact with their friends – for example *Scramble*, *Scrabble* or *Bowling* – or interact with total strangers – such as *Farm Town* or *FarmVille*. *Facebook* also provides the user with a wall, the option to update their status and the ability to comment on other users' walls and status updates, which is similar to *MySpace's* comments and blurb functions. When a user logs into *Facebook* they are taken to the homepage, which allows them to update their status as well as read the 'newsfeed', which contains their friends' updates, highlights and requests. The user can then click on their own profile. This network allows the user to have a profile to socialise with 'friends' as well as the ability to 'play' with the various applications and meet other users. The applications also allow you to add your *Facebook* friends so all elements of the site are tethered to social interaction. *Facebook* encourages multiple levels of social networking as well as interaction with the network itself. Status updates, wall comments, photographs, chat, quizzes and games all reveal the user's *Facebook* history and develop their digital presence. As with *MySpace*, this digital presence is always online. All the information that is uploaded to the site can be commented on, whether the user is there or not. The identity of the user might be given briefly or in-depth, but it works to create the profile. The interactions within the network itself are what develop the user's digital presence, a presence which is inextricable from other areas of the user's life.

Compared with *MySpace* and *Facebook*, *twitter* is a simple online social network, which is based on the question: 'What are you doing?'[44] *Twitter* differs from *MySpace* and *Facebook* in that it is a microblogging service. It works on constant status updates known as tweets, which cannot be longer than 140 characters. Similar to the other two networks, the user creates a profile, but like the tweets, this profile is also brief – name, location, web address and biography. The user is also only allowed one picture, so the profile is kept very small, with the central focus of the service being on the blog. Although *twitter* has effectively been around since 2006, it was not until early 2009 that it really began to gain broad popularity. I suggest this can be linked to the number of celebrities using the service. Unlike fanpages or private celebrity profiles, twitterers can 'follow' the updates of celebrities. This obviously raises concerns regarding privacy and fraudulent users, which is something that I discuss, in relation to celebrities, in Chapter three. As a social network, *twitter*, which does allow photographs (twitpics), video and music (via such services as blip.fm) to be linked to, is a pared-down version of *MySpace* and *Facebook*. The bells and whistles have been removed and it largely comes down to communicating thoughts and ideas. Within these constant updates, what you ate for breakfast becomes more important than where you went to school ... unless that is what you are tweeting about. *Twitter* is based on the everyday activities of the user, however mundane they might be. It is an example of a development in social networking where the sole purpose is short but constant updates of what the user has been doing offline. As with the other networks, the information disclosed in profiles is there to create a user identity and it is the interactions of the user with the network that develops the user's digital presence.

In his introduction to *The Conflict in Modern Culture and Other Essays*, Simmel writes:

> Life, as we have said can manifest itself only in particular forms; yet, owing to its essential restlessness, life constantly struggles against its own products, which have become fixed and do not move along with it. This process manifests itself as the displacement of an old form by a new one. This constant change in the content of culture, even of whole culture styles, is the sign of the infinite fruitfulness of life. At the same time, it marks the deep contradiction between life's eternal flux and the objective validity and authenticity of the forms through which it proceeds. It moves constantly between death and resurrection – between resurrection and death.[45]

The Internet demonstrates a change in culture, and participation within social networks (such as MMORPGs, online dating wesbsites, blogs and social networking sites) illustrates a change in cultural styles of communication. *MySpace*, *Facebook* and *twitter* differ in content, structure and audience but their purpose is the same – social networking. Certain 'About Me' information is required so that a user can create a digital presence. Social networks are organisms inside of which are a multitude of digital presences. Simmel suggests that 'the inner necessity of organic evolution is far profounder than the necessity that a wound-up spring will be released'.[46] Social networks seem to have both organic and inorganic qualities, hence my categorisation of them as social organisms. How the social network organism affects a user's 'life' is recognised in the relationship with their digital presence therein. This occurs by the movement from identity creation, through the disclosure of 'About Me' information, to using and developing a digital presence by action within the network. In relation to screen actors, Benjamin argues that the 'performance is not a single entity; it consists of many individual performances'.[47] The performances and actions of a user through their digital presence build, mould and shape it, allowing us to see the two-fold relationship between user and digital presence.

Notes

1. Kent, M. (2005) *The Invisible Empire: Border Protection on the Electronic Frontier*. Murdoch, Western Australia: Murdoch University, p. 179.
2. Wachowksi, A. & Wachowski, L. (1999) *The Matrix*. USA: Groucho II Film Partnership.

3. See Surratt, C. (1998) *Netlife: Internet Citizens and their Communities*, New York: Nova Science; Turkle, S. (1995) *Life on the Screen: Identity in the Age of the Internet.* New York: Simon & Schuster; Waskul, D. & Jones, S. (2003) *Self-Games and Body-Play: Personhood in Online Chat and Cybersex.* New York: Peter Lang.

4. Zhao, S. (2009) 'The digital self: through the looking glass of telecopresent others', *Symbolic Interaction*, 28(3): 388.

5. Turkle, *op. cit.*, p. 10.

6. Benjamin, W. (2008) *The Work of Art in the Age of Mechanical Reproduction.* London: Penguin Books, pp. 17–18.

7. Wu, J., Li, P. & Rao, S. (2008) 'Why they enjoy virtual game worlds? An empirical investigation', *Journal of Electronic Commerce Research*, 9(3): 221.

8. World of Warcraft Game Guide (2009) 'What is World of Warcraft?', available at: *http://www.worldofwarcraft.com/info/basics/guide.html* (accessed 13 June 2009).

9. *Ibid.*

10. *Ibid.*

11. Kock, N. (2008) 'E-Collaboration and E-Commerce in virtual worlds: the potential of Second Life and World of Warcraft', *International Journal of e-Collaboration*, 4(3): 2.

12. World of Warcraft Game Guide (2009) 'Party etiquette', available at: *http://www.worldofwarcraft.com/info/basics/partyrules.html* (accessed 13 June 2009).

13. Eve-Online (2009) available at: *www.EVE-Online.com* (accessed 13 June 2009).

14. This is with the exception of those playing in China. China has a separate server where they do not allow players to podkill.

15. Eve-Online, *op. cit.*

16. Evelopedia (2009) 'Griefing', available at: *http://wiki.eveonline.com/wiki/Griefing* (accessed 13 June 2009).

17. *Ibid.*

18. Simmel, G. (1968) K. P. Etztkorn (trans) *The Conflict in Modern Culture and Other Essays.* New York: Teachers College Press, p. 92.

19. Second Life (2009) 'Frequently asked questions', available at *http://secondlife.com/whatis/faq.php#01* (accessed 15 June 2009).

20. Second Life (2009) 'The creations', available at: *http://secondlife.com/whatis/creations.php.* (accessed 17 June 2009).

21. Boyes, E. (2009) 'I live out my sexual fantasy as an online escort', available at: *http://au.greenpixels.com/articles/features/2256/I-live-out-my-sexual-fantasy-as-an-online-escort* (accessed 17 June 2009).

22. Boyes E. (2009) 'My real-life husband doesn't know about my Second Life one', available at: *http://au.greenpixels.com/articles/features/2143/My-real-life-husband-doesnt-know-about-my-Second-Life-one* (accessed 17 June 2009).

23. *Ibid.*

24. Meadows, M.S. (2008) *I, Avatar: The Culture and Consequences of Having a Second Life.* Berkeley, CA: New Riders, p. 8.

25. Second Life Grid (2009) 'Real work gets done in virtual worlds', *http://secondlifegrid.net/* (accessed 17 June 2009).

26. This does bring into question the idea of being on- and offline. This is something that will be discussed in later chapters.
27. Boyes, E. 'My real-life husband doesn't know about my Second Life one', *op. cit.*
28. We are again seeing the boundaries of on/offline blurred as questions regarding virtual marriages and fidelity arise. Is virtual marriage part of role-playing within the game? Is it infidelity? Or does it come down to intent? When the distinction between on/offline environments become joined, what we once believed about these relationships are called into question.
29. Jenkins, H. (2006) *Fans, Bloggers and Gamers.* New York: New York University Press, p. 174.
30. *Ibid.*
31. Gunter, B. (2008) 'Internet dating: a British survey,' *Aslib Proceedings,* 60(2): 96.
32. Jenkins, *op. cit.*
33. de Laat, P.B. (2008) 'Online diaries: reflections on trust, privacy, and exhibitionism', *Ethics and Information Technology,* 10:57, 59.
34. MacDougall, R. (2005) 'Identity, electronic ethos, and blogs: a technologic analysis of symbolic exchange on the new news medium', *The American Behavioral Scientist,* 49(4): 575.
35. Some texts state 1996, but the majority state 1997.
36. Gaither, Chris (2003) 'Six Degrees Co', available at: *http://www.boston.com/business/globe/articles/2003/12/07/six_degrees_co/12/7/2003* (accessed 25 June 2009); boyd, D.M. & Ellison, N. (2007) 'Social network sites: definition, history, and scholarship', *Journal of Computer-Mediated Communication,* 13(1), available at: *http://jcmc.indiana.edu/vol13/issue1/boyd.ellison.html* (accessed 18 June 2009).
37. *Ibid.*
38. *Ibid.*
39. *Ibid.*
40. Beer, D. (2008) 'Social network(ing) sites – revisiting the story so far: a response to Danah Boyd & Nicole Ellison', *Journal of Computer-Mediated Communication,* 13(2): 518.
41. boyd, D.M. & Ellison, N., *op. cit.*
42. Lahlou, S. (2008) 'Identity, social status, privacy and face-keeping in digital society', *Social Science Information,* 47(3): 310.
43. MySpace (2009) 'Today on MySpace', available at: *http://au.myspace.com/* (accessed 26 June 2009).
44. Twitter (2009) available at: *https://twitter.com/* (accessed 26 June 2009).
45. Simmel, *op. cit.,* p. 12.
46. Simmel, *op. cit.,* p. 28.
47. Benjamin, *op. cit.,* p. 20.

3

All a *twitter*: celebrities and social networking

In 2008 I signed up to *twitter* as a research exercise for this book. I wanted to try a range of different online social networks in order to work out how they functioned and what their purpose was. I signed up, posted a few tweets, added a couple of my friends, but found the whole process a bit lonely as I felt that I was microblogging to no one in particular. So I left my fledgling *twitter* account and went back to *Facebook*, where according to my friend count, I was quite popular. Then my favourite comedian, Russell Brand, issued a video message on *Facebook* to follow him on *twitter*.[1] I logged into *twitter* and started following Brand, as well as a number of other celebrities. My *twitterverse* had developed into pages of updates about the lives of famous people, by famous people; well this is what I assumed. I witnessed the banter between celebrities and their replies to their fans, hoping that one day I would also be at the end of one of them.[2] I had indeed been sold by the idea that these people I admired were only one tweet away.

The formation of celebrity on social network sites is powerful. This chapter explores how the digital presence of celebrities impacts on their lives and the lives of fans/followers. The relationship between celebrity and these networks is two-fold: celebrity participation and celebrity creation. In the context of this debate, I define actual celebrities as those who were already famous offline. The relationship between the social network and the celebrity is highly visible, which makes them a convenient and pertinent subject for discussion. I first discuss celebrity participation, and the way that actual celebrities interact with these websites. The chapter investigates the reciprocal flow of information between the celebrity and *MySpace*, *Facebook* and *twitter*. This exploration also looks at fraudulent celebrity profile creation and the way that these 'fake' accounts impact on a celebrity's real identity.

Anyone can create a user profile, so it can be difficult to verify the authenticity of the account, and for this reason identity is a significant part of this discussion. The relationship between celebrities and networks illustrates how social networks can impact on the user's life. This leads us to a discussion regarding the creation of the 'net-celebrity'.

The second part of this chapter looks at celebrity creation within social networks: generating the net-celebrity. This discussion commences with a look at *Facebook* social climbing through an interview with Jeffrey Scott Shapiro. Moving on from this discussion, based on becoming famous by friend count or friend type, I approach the different forms of net-celebrity. These are the self-made and celebrity-created net-celebrities. Self-made net-celebrities, in the context of this book, are users who developed their celebrity status by their participation on these networks. This chapter looks at a number of examples from those made famous for posting party invitations on *MySpace* to those bands that have been touted as *MySpace* successes. I also look at celebrity-created net-celebrities (users who have had a 'famous' helping hand in creating their celebrity status), using the Bryan Brinkman Experiment. Celebrity creation and the idea of the net-celebrity is an important part of the social network machine. The spillage of information from the pages of social networking sites into the public lives of celebrities exemplifies the doubt that can be cast on any perceived 'split' between online and offline activity.

Sycophants and imposters

Celebrity participation in social networks is a powerful marketing tool as well as useful for solidifying a fan-base. It could be argued that these two are one and the same, but such an argument would be ignoring the 'personal' side to Internet relationships that social networking sites are generally used for, such as status updates, microblogging, video messages and so on. The way that celebrities actually participate in social networks is dependent on the format of the site. Each network has particular ways celebrities can interact with their fans (including fan pages, groups or user pages), the structure of which determines the nature of the interaction. The importance of authenticating identity is emphasised in the context of these differing forms of digital celebrity presence.

Celebrity pages on *MySpace* work in a similar fashion to many celebrity fan sites. These pages can be set up both by celebrities and by fans. *Facebook* has group pages as well as user profiles, and like non-celebrities, most celebrities keep their personal *Facebook* profiles private. *Facebook* has recently restructured its 'group' pages to look more like standard user accounts, and some celebrities, Noel Fielding[3] for example, use the status update function in their 'group' account like standard profiles, and answer the insipid *Facebook* question of 'what's on your mind?' Status updates and blogs are the key elements of these pages as they allow fans to be privy to the celebrity's life. Nayor asserts that 'the culture of celebrity, as we know, thrives on sustained interest in the private lives behind the public faces of the star. That is, we are curious about what they are in secret, away from the media glare.'[4] Celebrities using group pages on *Facebook* and *MySpace* participate by the status update, blog/note functions and video messages. Musicians use *MySpace* to give fans tasters of their new music, and, in recent history, for album launches.[5] Fan/group profiles on *Facebook* and *MySpace* are structured in such a way that there are still barriers between the fan and the celebrity. Fans can write on the 'wall' of the profile and *MySpace* also allows the user to send private messages. These celebrity pages tend to be specifically focused on showcasing the talent of the celebrity, by sharing their latest music, films or performances, so a social barrier is maintained in exchanges between fan and celebrity. These pages seem to encourage the fan to engage with the celebrity's work and other fans, rather than with the celebrities themselves. However, the social network *twitter* works on a very different premise.

Twitter, as a microblogging service, is focused on the 140-character tweet. Tweets play an important role in generating interest in the celebrity on *twitter* and are also a way of interacting directly with fans. Fan and group pages on *Facebook* and *MySpace* focus on the career of the celebrity, whereas *twitter* concentrates on the everyday life of the celebrity. Although some celebrities run their account using a public relations officer or team, the majority of famous twitterers are tweeting for themselves. If they have someone tweet on their behalf this is disclosed or is quite obvious. Puente reveals 'some celebrity Twitterers – Britney Spears, 50 Cent, Kanye West, Barack Obama – have ghostwriters to supply their tweets because they're too busy'.[6] In my experience it would seem that the majority of celebrities tweet for themselves as a way to connect with their fans.[7] A large number of celebrities participate in this culture with regular updates and some connect with their fans more than others. Puente cites the example of Demi Moore, an avid *twitter* user, saving one fan from suicide. 'A chain of tweets involving Demi Moore led to police preventing a San Jose woman from harming herself after she sent the actress message that read like suicide notes.'[8] Moore's fans contacted the police on reading the post.[9] The interaction between fans/celebrities and fans/fans on *twitter* is unique because it gives insight into the everyday aspect of a celebrity's life in what might be described as acceptable voyeurism. Although it could be argued that tweeting is just like sending an email or fan letter, it is not. There are distinct barriers between celebrity and fan when considering email, fan mail or even a contribution to a fan forum. However, communication with celebrities on *twitter* is far more immediate. A strategic fan can see when a celebrity is online, send their tweet accordingly and eagerly await a response. There is no limit to the amount of people you can follow, so potentially a fan could spend their leisure time rubbing digital shoulders with their heroes as the replies roll in. Lee and Scott write that 'it is logical to view celebrities as a source of leisure activity or product. A celebrity can become a powerful object of leisure involvement for some fans.'[10] *Twitter* has added a new dimension to this leisure activity. It weakens the communication barrier between fans and their idols. Fans can follow celebrities, and vice versa, but this function can be manipulated.

Non-celebrities often set up and manage the 'fan pages' on networks such as *Facebook* and *MySpace*. This is also the case for celebrity user profiles on networks such as *Facebook* and *twitter*. Many fraudulent account holders make no attempt to disguise themselves as the real celebrity.[11] Owners of faux celebrity accounts, disclosed and undisclosed, tend to use social networks as a form of parody, or to create faux-blogs for celebrities that they admire or dislike. Phweeters (phony tweeters) often have numerous (and loyal) fans. There are also those fraudulent account holders who pretend to be celebrities, unsurprisingly creating difficulties for the real person. In relation to this topic Coyle remarks that:

> ... concerns have been raised about users' privacy. Last month a prankster gained access to the accounts of several high-profile twitterers including Obama and singer Britney Spears, posting obscene updates under their names.[12]

Websites such as *valebrity*[13] attempt to identify 'real' celebrity accounts and there are multiple websites dedicated to uncovering fraudulent users. Social networks try and crack down on misuse by having policies and procedures to deal with these situations.[14] *Twitter* now has the option of having a user account verified, so other users can identify the profile as that of the real person – namely celebrities. This leads into the subject of identity verification.

I asserted, in Chapter two, that certain 'About Me' information such as name, age and profession are the foundation for a user's identity. This identity, coupled with the actions (posts, tweets, photographs, video, comments) of a user, results in the creation of a digital presence. When this digital presence is that of a celebrity, the actions of this digital presence are emphasised. Those on the verge of becoming celebrities are examples of how the digital presence, which is grounded in the user's offline experiences, can impact on how the user is perceived on *and* offline. Australian Olympic swimmer Stephanie Rice's meteoric rise to stardom was coloured by stories regarding her *Facebook* profile. Rice's profile, which was not private at the time of her ascent into celebrity, contained images of herself posing suggestively in raunchy costumes. As Angela Saurine wrote, 'happy snaps of Stephanie Rice partying have been deemed too raunchy for Swimming Australia, with all of the swimmers ordered to block public access to their Facebook profile pages'.[15] News outlets and Swimming Australia chastised Rice for this behaviour given her high visibility and 'role model' status. Photographs like those of Rice indicate that there are, what I refer to as, everyday undercurrents present in social networks that negatively affect a user's life. Celebrities are highly visible and this allows us to see how undercurrents such as photographs and status updates impact on other areas of the user's life. A lack of, or confused, context often surrounds network contents such as photographs and status updates. When these are then taken out of the network altogether issues can ensue.

As the popularity of *twitter* increases, some journalists and writers are selecting comments from online social networks as news material. Predominantly these updates are being used for entertainment gossip stories; for example, *USA Today* recently published a story about the 'tech' habits of celebrities.[16] However, this practice becomes troublesome when random 'updates' are used out of context. A trend is occurring in online news where the research material has been taken from celebrity social network pages. Many stories are in good fun; Ashton Kutcher, for example, made the entertainment news when he used *twitter* to make a claim to pulling a prank on his wife Demi Moore.[17] Material is also used to follow celebrity relationships; John Mayer's tweets were used as evidence of his breakup with Jennifer Anniston. Ultimately these 'updates' are used to create tabloid news. Nayor proposes:

> That part of the aura of celebrity is not simply transgression but the very idea and practice of excess, such as excessive drinking, scandalous deeds, wealth, power, good looks and lifestyle. The exaggerated, dramatic and hyper-visible descriptions and depictions of celebrities is linked, I suggest, to the excesses that they are expected to have.[18]

This occurred when musician Lily Allen's *Facebook* comments were used to declare that she was suicidal. The excess and 'secrets' revealed in tweets and status updates are easy fodder for entertainment news stories, and little or no context is provided when comments are used. This (mis)use of tweets or status updates shows how these types of communication are everyday undercurrents within the network. The lack of context allows constant opportunities for these messages to be misread. Context is an important factor here. At this point it is necessary to clarify my position regarding context in relation to social networks. The length and limited number of characters (on both *twitter* and *Facebook*) available for single status updates means that context for these posts is also limited. When updates are removed from networks altogether, their context is lost entirely. The ebbs and flows of everyday life become magnified when revealed by a celebrity. These banal and often random utterances affect a celebrity's digital presence and have become another aspect of their life that is scrutinised by entertainment news outlets. For example, a Russell Brand story that was posted on news.com.au in the *Showbuzz* section cited a tweet by Brand declaring his desire for a new form of cereal. They stated that:

> RUSSELL Brand wants a breakfast cereal made of cigarettes. The TV presenter would love to start his morning with an unhealthy combination of cereal, jam, chocolate and deadly nicotine sticks.
>
> Writing on his Twitter page, Brand said: 'I demand a new breakfast cereal called "Lucky Fags" – honey-nut clusters, with chocolate, jam sandwiches and cigarettes in it – GOOD MORNING!' – BANG Showbiz/Reuters.[19]

Brand's tweet was taken out of context. In a *twitter* message directing Brand to this article, he responded: 'I saw that. It's mental. Obviously, I would not endorse a cigarette infused cereal.'[20] Followers of Brand's *twitter* account would know this. Others, despite the ridiculous nature of the news story, may think differently.[21] Celebrity accounts are being used for entertainment news fodder multiple times a week on websites such as news.com.au.[22] This re-posting, out of context, moves beyond the social network. It not only influences the celebrity's digital presence but also how they are perceived in other areas of their life.

Given that the author of the 'updates' cannot always be identified, questions concerning the legitimacy of using posts as 'direct quotes' start to appear. An example is the assault case between R&B musicians Rihanna and Chris Brown. Five days after the assault took place, it was reported by various media outlets that Chris Brown, in reference to Rihanna, wrote 'you'll begin to see her true colors. Believe it!'[23] on his (private) *Facebook* page and changed his relationship status to single. Brown's public relations team then issued the following statement on 15 February 2009:

> Much of what has been speculated or reported on blogs and/or reported in the media is wrong. While I would like to be able to talk about this more, until the legal issues are resolved, this is all I can say except that I have not written any messages or made any posts to Facebook, on blogs or any place else. Those posts or writings under my name are frauds.[24]

The Chris Brown and Rihanna case not only highlights the need for faux celebrity profiles to be monitored, but is also a prime example of how a user's digital presence can affect other aspects of their life. Online social networks are becoming a pool of free information on which tabloid journalism is thriving. Alongside this, however, are cases of actual networking among journalists, which is discussed in an interview with Jeffrey Scott Shapiro in the following section of this chapter.

I bet you look good on the dancefloor...[47]

The goal of becoming a celebrity and the requirement of (at least) 15 minutes of fame is an objective that has become ingrained into modern British, American and Australian cultures. Oliver James, discussing the contemporary condition of fame-lust, writes:

> Today, even the most talentless, unattractive and impoverished people hanker after such prizes. The process has been rapidly accelerated by so-called reality TV programmes such as *Big Brother* which purport to provide a democratic opportunity for anyone at all to become famous ...[25]

James argues that many cultures[26] are suffering from the 'Affluenza Virus', which 'entails placing a high value on acquiring money and possessions, looking good in the eyes of others and wanting to be famous'.[27] This obsession with becoming famous has skyrocketed in the past decade with the 'talent' juggernaut of *Idol*, *X Factor* and *So You Think You Can Dance?*. There has also been the *Big Brother* phenomenon and *Biggest Loser* series. A number of these programmes are based on the ability to perform, *Big Brother* is based on just being and the *Biggest Loser* on being overweight. These programmes are all part of the 'reality' genre, fuelled by wannabe celebrities. The exposure provided by these programmes gives the participants a chance at fame, but they have to overcome a number of hurdles – contests/battles/isolation/exercise – in order to get there. Those who want fame without such hoopla go to the free-for-all terrain of the Internet.

The Internet provides a space where the technologically literate can attempt to become stars. Robin reminds us that, 'in the virtual world, it is suggested, we shall receive all the gratifications that we are entitled to, but have been deprived of; in this world, we can reclaim the (infantile) illusion of magical creative power'.[28] *Youtube* has provided those with something to say and a video camera somewhere to upload their creative endeavours. Brook 'Brookers' Brodack, famous for her comedy and parody videos on *Youtube*, was the first official star to crossover from the Internet to television. Carson Daly, host of American late night show *Last Call with Carson Daly*, signed Brodack in 2006. There have been many notable *Youtube* celebrities, whose videos attract many hits and their viral messages have legions of fans.[29] They are what I refer to as net-celebrities. They operate from bedrooms and family backyards. They are based on raw talent or lack thereof, but they are doing it with a central purpose, namely to be seen. *Youtube* has been a powerful vehicle for the sharing of new talent, information and the rise of the net-celebrity. The *Youtube* community could be classified as an online social network, but it does not fall within the category of those that are the particular focus of this book. The group of social networks that are under scrutiny do, however, play a comparable role in the creation of net-celebrities.

Similar to *Youtube*, other online social networks including *Facebook*, *Bebo* and *MySpace* have their own net-celebrities. Many net-celebrities on *Facebook* are regarded as such due to their friend count or the notoriety of their friends, so they are famous purely for social networking. Jeffrey Scott Shapiro, a journalist and lawyer from Washington, DC, explores the idea of social climbing in 'Confessions of a Facebook Social Climber'. He begins with the comment, 'I recently became friends with Charlie Sheen – but not exactly. It's a little complicated. You see, I've spent the past three months moving up the Facebook social ladder, "friending" more and more important people every day.'[30] As a known journalist, Shapiro was in a unique position in his challenge of networking himself up the *Facebook* social ladder. Intrigued by what seemed to be a social experiment, I interviewed Shapiro about the reasons behind this exploration of social mobility.

Angela Thomas-Jones: When you commenced your Facebook social climbing, did you view it as a kind of social experiment?

Jeffrey Scott Shapiro: No. I'm a journalist who likes to connect with people of interest and I quickly began to realise that Facebook was an excellent way to reach out to people directly that I would typically have to go through a press representative to get to.

ATJ: So, then what was the purpose of it?

JSS: A journalist is only as valuable as his sources. The more interesting people you have a pipeline to, the more options you have when you need information or an interview.

ATJ: Which is interesting because that is how I contacted you. So, what did you hope to gain from it?

JSS: Aside from gaining sources, I think I was intrigued with the fact I could reach out to important and interesting people so easily. Once I connected with the Bush family through Pierce, I was curious to see who else I could connect with. It was almost like going to a library for the first time. You find a great book and say to yourself, wow, if I was able to get this book for free, I wonder what else is out there?

ATJ: Do you think the notoriety of you and some of your offline friends helped to secure some of your Facebook celebrity 'friends'?

JSS: Absolutely. There's no question that my own ability to send people links to published pieces I'd written helped my status when contacting them and when I had some celebrity friends it helped me gain others. People always assume you're important if other important people recognise you and they either suspect you can be of use to them somehow or you're someone they don't want to turn down – then they might be out of the loop.

ATJ: What, do you believe, is the role of online social networks in our everyday lives?

JSS: I think online social networks can be a wonderful way to connect with people easily that would otherwise be difficult to contact, but it can also be worthless if you connect with too many people. There are some people I know who have so many Facebook friends that they can't even keep up with who they know and so the term being someone's 'friend' loses meaning. One member of a prestigious political family once joked with me about this issue. I told him when finally meeting him in person that I'd sent him a friend request and he smiled and answered, 'Yeah, I know, but I'm still thinking about it. I have to see how many friends you have because if it's too many then I don't feel very special, I assume that I'm just another number.' Eventually, he accepted my friend request. For that reason, however, I try to keep my Facebook friends limited to people I actually communicate with or could have a reason to. One rule of thumb I have is to accept all journalists who contact me.

ATJ: Why do people attempt to climb the social network ladder?

JSS: I think some people like myself legitimately want to expand their contact base, especially if they're in journalism, politics or even business. Other people want to feel more important than they do or they're looking for a fun way to pass the time while at their day job.

ATJ: Having had personal experience with online social networks and celebrity, what role do social network sites such as Twitter, Facebook and MySpace play in the lives of celebrities and their fans? In relation to this, how important is it for 'celebrities' to be a part of these networks and get involved with their fans?

JSS: When I exposed one major fake celebrity profile for not being real, his publicist immediately had it removed. Then, after trying to have more fake celebrity profiles removed, he talked with his best clients and decided to stop. 'We came to realize there's only one thing worse than having a fake celebrity profile on Facebook,' he told me, 'and that's NOT having one out there in your name. It means you're no longer hot and that people don't really care about you anymore.' I think some celebrities, especially those comedians who are looking to draw crowds for their acts, are using some of these sites successfully and others who don't need a following like that, movie stars like Reese Witherspoon, don't need to.

Shapiro's interview was revealing for several reasons. Although his intentions are, to a large extent, related to business networking, there is also the added intrigue of discovering who else is 'out there'. For journalists trying to write a story, these networks potentially remove boundaries for contacting those who might otherwise be out of reach. This resonates with my earlier assertion that social networks are reformulating the avenues of contact with celebrities. Whereas 'fans' use it to contact their heroes, journalists are using *Facebook* as another resource for work. Shapiro's use of *Facebook* to obtain contacts differs from the way in which tweets on *twitter* are used as stories. This may have a lot to do with the way in which participation on these websites operates. Celebrity accounts on *Facebook* (non-fan pages) are usually private and require the acceptance of friend requests. By contrast, on *twitter*, the majority of celebrity accounts are open, and material can be taken straight from them without the permission of the author.

A distinction can be made between types of social climbing within these networks. There is social climbing for the sake of becoming popular, where status is drawn from the amount of friends you have, as well as social climbing relating to the types of friends you have. Shapiro highlights this when addressing the nature of 'friend'ship. Social climbing can create celebrity due to the popularity or friend count of the user or can be created by the user's links with celebrities (which is how Shapiro was able to attract certain celebrities to his list). The appropriation of celebrity in fake user accounts that Shapiro touches on is particularly thought-provoking. Fake accounts are an indication of popularity, but because of the potential for negative publicity (as in the Chris Brown case) they are an aspect of the celebrity's digital presence that needs to be monitored by the celebrity.

On *MySpace*, similarly to *Facebook*, there are net-celebrities who have become popular because of their 'social' network status and friendships, and there are those famous for their talent. An example is provided by Australian party boy Corey Delaney/Worthington. In January 2008, 16-year-old Worthington took his *MySpace* popularity offline when he posted an open party invitation to his 'friends'. Worthington caused outrage in Australia and received worldwide news coverage, when more than 500 attendees at the party damaged his parents' house and neighbouring properties. Worthington's (un)popularity continued when he neglected to show any remorse for his antics. His attitude towards the party, and his parents, resulted in him being labelled 'teen brat' and a 'Gen Z poster boy' by the media. It also resulted in a host of copycat 'Corey' parties.[31] He was signed by manager Max Markson and offered a host of DJ gigs. In mid 2008 he entered the *Big Brother* house as an intruder and was also allegedly trying to secure the rights to the Beastie Boys hit 'Fight For Your Right to Party'. There was a post-Corey backlash by the Internet community with websites including *http://www.slapcorey.com/* and *YouTube* clips criticising his behaviour. The fact that Worthington's notoriety was born from the Internet brought to light the power and real world impact of the 'social' network organism. Social networks do not exist in an ethereal cyber-bubble and are not unconnected to offline activity. For this reason the net-celebrity phenomenon, albeit often brief, is very real. Worthington was a brattish anti-hero for a few months, but like so many net-celebrities, his Internet bravado did not translate into the offline world. British teenager Gemma Anscomb found her fame in a similar manner[32] by advertising her party on *Bebo*. Her small sleepover garnered media attention when it turned into a drug-fuelled party. Ecstasy was given to the family pet[33] and the parents were left with a £5000 repair bill. The Anscomb story, likened to Worthington's, was spread through newspapers and online news networks. Anscomb relished in her 15 minutes of fame, before being relegated to relative anonymity. This form of net-celebrity status, while fleeting, impacts on the user's digital presence and in turn other aspects of their life. Worthington made Australian news again in 2009 when it was discovered that he had joined the workforce.[34] This form of net-celebrity is only labelled as such due to the nature of its initiation. Although it may begin on the Internet it is often quickly quashed once attempts are made to extend it offline. Fame on these networks, while influenced by the number of friends or followers a user has, does not have to be achieved by throwing an outlandish party.

MySpace celebrity Chris Crocker achieved worldwide attention when he posted his 'Leave Britney Alone' video on *MySpace* (over 3 million hits) and *YouTube* (over 24 million hits). This clip has since been turned into parodies – including one by actor Seth Green. Crocker's *MySpace* video channel, which consists of short recordings on various subjects, has over 50,000 subscribers and over 49 million hits. Crocker has since appeared on Jimmy Kimmell's late-night talk show, and *Variety* stated that '44 Blue Prods. has inked a development deal with Chris Crocker'.[35] However, in a *YouTube* video released in April 2008, Crocker states that due to censorship issues, he would not be participating in any show or website deal.[36] According to Crocker's website he is now working on his music career. His songs are available on his *MySpace* page, which includes videos, links to music and merchandise available for purchase. Crocker has switched between *YouTube* and *MySpace* to cement his status as a popular net-celebrity. Although he has been given the opportunity to go offline, he has remained online in the arena that has made him famous. This fame seems to be that of his digital presence. Keeping 'fame' on the Internet seems to be the key in sustaining the status of the net-celebrity. Tila Tequila, who is discussed later, provides a prime example of this. *MySpace* has been linked to the rise in popularity of musicians such as Lily Allen and the Arctic Monkeys and for this reason it is an area where the creation of the net-celebrity holds resonance.

MySpace's music section is what differentiates it from other social networks such as *twitter* and *Facebook*. The music profiles feature an array of musicians from the already famous to those who are trying to launch their careers. The music section's 'Top Artists' are split into unsigned, independent and major. At a glance you can flip between the top music from these categories by country. It is, however, confusing that famous artists such as Fat Boy Slim, The Darkness, daft punk, Jimmy Eat World and Cypress Hill can be found in the unsigned acts category. Nevertheless *MySpace* is a solid forum for musicians to be heard. Although popularity and celebrity can be accomplished and sustained on these networks, very few acts have taken popularity initiated on *MySpace* offline. Lily Allen's links with the network is an example of an exception to this precedent. Allen actually obtained a record deal prior to her *MySpace* success, but *MySpace* is acknowledged as the way in which she garnered attention and allowed her to establish a significant fan-base.[37] *MySpace* thus plays an important role in sustaining those lesser-known celebrities who already have one foot in the door.

The story of Tila Tequila is an example of *MySpace* fuelling an aspiring celebrity's career. In 2006 *Playboy* model Tila Tequila was touted as *MySpace* Queen and appeared as the most successful person to come out of the unsigned artists category because of her number of hits. These hits on her profile provide access to her music as well as an array of scantily clad pictures, explaining why critics have had issues with this popularity being solely related to her music. Pop critic Jonah Weiner questioned the 'musical democracy' of *MySpace*:

> In these early days of MySpace, it's naive to think that the artists who benefit most from the site's buzz will differ markedly from those at the top of the pop charts. Despite the Internet's many decentralizing effects on musical authority, it's natural that the millions of kids whose tastes are still informed by MTV and commercial radio are going to click to bands similar to those they already like. So far, the genre that MySpace has helped most concretely is emo-punk … Like grunge and nu-metal before it, emo is the current soundtrack to American white adolescent angst: a perfect fit for the site's legion of computer-owning 15-year-olds.[38]

But in 2006 *MySpace* fans were more than just 15 year olds. Comscore's press release in October 2006 showed that 12–17 year olds made up only 11.9 per cent of the audience. It revealed that 18–34 year olds were 34.8 per cent and 35–54 year olds were 40.6 per cent of the audience.[39] This document revealed not only a growth in usage but also an increase in age range of users from 2005 to 2006, seemingly making it a prominent place to be heard. Weiner's sentiments are corroborated by the fact that few unsigned talents have made it offline. *MySpace* plays an important role in garnering attention for signed/known talent and can also provide net-celebrity status. Unlike Worthington and Anscomb, musicians/bands come to *MySpace* with a talent and are looking for sustained exposure, rather than 15 minutes of fame. For this reason, maintaining and evolving a digital presence is of great importance. Uploading music, album launches and updating blogs work to develop this presence and attract an audience. The audience is far reaching and there are opportunities for unsigned acts to gain a certain level of success. The accounts of those bands whose success has been linked to *MySpace*, however, do not necessarily tell the full story.

One famous case of *MySpace* being linked to the success of a band is that of the Arctic Monkeys. The band began playing together in 2001 and the rapid nature of their success has been attributed to the Internet – namely peer-to-peer sharing of music by fans. Their biography on *RollingStone* states:

> They began playing locally in mid-2003 and soon began handing out CD-R demos to fans, who took it upon themselves to file-share the songs. This in turn bolstered Arctic Monkeys' fan base, which was further consolidated when the music was uploaded onto a fan-created MySpace page for the band.[40]

In late 2005, the band's single, 'I Bet You Look Good on the Dancefloor,' went to number one on the UK charts before an album had been released. Their debut album released in January 2006, *Whatever People Say I Am, That's What I'm Not*, became one of the fastest-selling British albums of all time, beating the first Oasis album as the biggest debut in UK rock history.[41] The success of the Arctic Monkeys is believed to have changed aspects of the music industry forever. Mark Binelli writes:

> When 'Dancefloor' debuted at Number One last year, it blindsided many in the British music industry and wildly excited others looking for a way to use the Internet to save the record business. 'It was completely accidental', Turner says. 'We never posted any songs ourselves.'
>
> 'We didn't do any promotion', adds Helders, who is wearing a bright-yellow T-shirt reading NO PROBLEM JAMAICA. 'There

were no posters around London. So newspapers and people like that thought, "What the fuck is this? Must be the Internet!" Well, the song's pretty good, too.'[42]

The Arctic Monkeys have been considered the epitome of Internet-made celebrities. They freely acknowledge that their fans 'made' them and that the Internet played a large role in their success. The Arctic Monkey's *MySpace* page is often attributed for this success. In an interview with *Prefix Magazine* in November 2005 the band mention their thoughts on this connection.

> PM: I notice you have a pretty popular site on Myspace.
>
> Arctic Monkeys: We don't know about that, either.
>
> PM: So that's not you guys?
>
> Arctic Monkeys: No, no. The other day someone said to us, 'I looked at your profile on Myspace.' I said, 'I don't even know what Myspace is.' [When we went number one in England] we were on the news and radio about how Myspace has helped us. But that's just the perfect example of someone who doesn't know what the fuck they're talking about. We actually had no idea what [Myspace] was.[43]

Although the Internet (in the form of peer-to-peer sharing of songs) played a significant role in the band's success, it is difficult to know whether an unknown *MySpace* page had the leading role in this celebrity creation. Today the band has official pages on both *Facebook* and *MySpace* with legions of fans on each, so the connection to these systems has obviously not hindered their success. Very few net-celebrities make the transition from these social networks and then maintain their status offline. Not that being an Internet celebrity is not a career in itself, as both Crocker and Tequila have proved. As Tequila says, 'This is my job ... That's how you maintain your popularity and keep it alive.'[44] Tila Tequila has made a career as an online social networking celebrity via her websites, fan-base, clothing line and music.

Net-celebrities do not have to be self-made; other celebrities can also create them. Through the use of social networking sites, website blogs and other media, celebrities can aid in celebrity creation by directing audience attention towards an unknown person. Oprah Winfrey and her 'book club' is a notable example of this. If your book appears on Oprah's book club, you are 'made'. A pertinent example of celebrity creation occurred on the Jimmy Fallon show. On 11 March 2009 *Late Night with Jimmy Fallon* host Jimmy Fallon and his guests, *DiggNation*'s Alex Albrecht and Kevin Rose, and comedian Russell Brand conducted a *twitter* experiment with one of the show's audience members – Bryan Brinkman. The purpose of the Bryan Brinkman Experiment was using *twitter* in an 'attempt to make an audience member bigger than Barrack Obama'.[45] Fallon and his guests put out a call on the show, via tweets on their *twitter* accounts and also through their individual websites for their followers to follow Bryan on *twitter*. Before the show had aired in the US Brinkman's number of followers had skyrocketed from seven to over 10,000. This experiment is an excellent example of the power of celebrity on these social networks, in terms of the ability of celebrities to create fame and the idea of celebrity creation. I conducted an email interview with Bryan, a week after the experiment commenced, about his feelings towards the experiment, online social networks and the idea of celebrity.

Angela Thomas-Jones: Before the Jimmy Fallon show, what was your opinion of Twitter and other online social networks? Were/are you on any other sites and how did you use these sites before the Jimmy Fallon Show?

Bryan Brinkman: Before the show I had dabbled into twitter for a few weeks before deciding it wasn't really worth it for me at the time. I didn't have any followers, and a handful of friends used it. I was already updating my status on facebook and blogging on tumblr, so I kinda pushed it aside and fed my other blogs through it. I used my tumblr to post general things that interested me, as well as art I made.

ATJ: On the show you said you had seven followers on Twitter, is this correct?

BB: It is 100% correct, I even made sure to capture proof before it skyrocketed. Ha ha.

ATJ: So, how did you get involved in the 'Experiment'?

BB: I had been planning on going to the show for weeks, and told my friends about it, one of whom works on the Late Night staff as an animator. Apparently they were throwing around the idea of having the DiggNation guys and Jimmy team up to make a audience member a twitter celebrity since combined they had half a million followers. When asked if the staff knew anybody coming to the show that day my name got mentioned and they called to ask if I had a twitter. I told them I kinda had one, but I didn't really have any friends on it, and they thought it would be perfect. They called me the night before the show to ask me about it, and then confirmed it was going to happen a few hours before the show, and the rest is on television.

ATJ: How did you feel about being involved in it? What was it like seeing your followers jump so significantly and how quickly did your followers jump?

BB: I was very reluctant at first; I'm a shy individual and the idea of being on television was terrifying. I remember constantly asking 'You're not going to embarrass me in front of the world right?'. After talking to the producers for a bit and realising it was a crazy opportunity for myself and my artwork, I agreed to do it. I remember as soon as they twittered at the live taping, the numbers shot up. It was over ten thousand before the show even aired, and jumped to over twenty thousand shortly afterwards. It was insane; I was in a panic because I was so unprepared for the mass amount of information flying at me. Dozens of emails and messages started pouring in immediately, and my website got thousands of hits. I went into a paranoid panic attack that night when I saw my name thrown around all over the web, it was so surreal.

ATJ: I myself followed you (I followed Russell's Brand suggestion to follow you) and I watched your numbers climb rapidly. You now have followers throughout the world and I was wondering, how has this experiment changed your online and offline life so far? How do you think it will affect other aspects of your life such as your video and cartoon career?

BB: It's definitely been a time-consumer this first week. I've always been connected through social networking sites, but adding twitter into the mix has been a huge addition. I'm much more aware of what's going on around the web involving myself and my story. Off line my life hasn't changed dramatically: I've been working during the day, and going out with friends in the evening. I'm trying to give myself breaks from twitter so it doesn't affect my relationships. It hasn't dramatically affected my career other then giving it a lot of publicity, but there's still plenty of time to see where things lead from here.

ATJ: How has this affected the traffic to your website [*http://www.brinkanimation.com*]?

BB: In the first week, the traffic on my site has increased 35,000 per cent. It has been amazing on a level that film festivals could never compare to.

ATJ: In relation to the experiment you say that it 'hasn't dramatically affected my career other then giving it a lot of publicity, but there's still plenty of time to see where things lead from here.' Do you think you'll use your exposure to try and further your career as a cartoonist?

BB: I do want to use the exposure to draw more attention to my personal art. It positively motivates me when I see so many people interested and enjoying what I create. As I show my art in progress, it will be exciting to get feedback in real time.

ATJ: I noticed in one of your tweets that you wrote 'every time i see a follower leave, its like a tiny dagger in my micro-blog heart. ill pour out a mini-forty for y'all, then i'll clean it up.' How do you feel about being thrust into celebritydom and having so many followers? Has your micro-blogging style or feelings towards these networks changed?

BB: That comment was made with a little sarcasm; with so many friends I really couldn't fret about a few people dropping me. Honestly I've taken the approach of just being myself, which to some people is probably very boring. The difference between myself and some of the other internet celebrities is that I was chosen to be famous for being a normal guy, and I don't want to try to be anything other than that. I'm still early in developing a style and voice to my writing, but I try my best to give people useful and interesting information. I've definitely grown to appreciate the twitter-verse; its much deeper than I first imagined.

ATJ: In relation to the 'twitter-verse' being deeper than you first imagined, what did you think about the purpose of twitter before the experiment?

BB: When I first started using twitter, it appeared to be similar to the 'Update Status' feature on social networking sites. After spending more time with it I learned the intricacies of the community. I found that the boundaries for creativity with it are limitless because you [sic] be anything you want it to.

ATJ: Having had personal experience with online social networks and celebrity, what role do social network sites such as twitter, Facebook and MySpace play in the lives of celebrities and their fans? In relation to this, how important is it for 'celebrities' to be a part of these networks and get involved with their fans?

BB: I think when a celebrity can interact with the fans on a level like twitter, it brings a much more human element to the mix. I think Jimmy Fallon is a perfect example: he's on television everyday, but he makes time for his fans and he appreciates them. He gets them involved, and it creates an interaction that transcends the show. I think it's very important for celebrities to show they are normal people that care about the fans that support them.

ATJ: Finally, from your own experience, how powerful is the role of 'celebrity' in these social networks in obtaining friends/followers? Do you agree that, in the context of online social networks, celebrity can create celebrity?

BB: Obviously it's easier for a celebrity to gain and influence followers. I'm a perfect example of that, and I try to do the same for people and things I appreciate. We are in an age of information sharing unlike ever before. In my case I became a celebrity for a moment; whether that moment has past or not, I still have the influence to share and connect with the people that have supported me so far. I think that's the greatest part of this: these followers made me. If they all left, I would just go back to the way things were.

The Bryan Brinkman Experiment and interview demonstrate how celebrity can create celebrity. They also show how digital presence impacts on the user and vice versa. These celebrities wanted to turn Brinkman into a 'rock star' and by asking their audience to follow him, they started to create a net-celebrity. Brinkman is aware that forms of celebrity creation can be fleeting and recognises that 'these followers made me'. He also recognises the important role that celebrity plays in building celebrity, by using his new found fame to 'pay it forward' by posting/tweeting about things that he himself appreciates – bands, art, TV programmes for example – as well as promoting his career as an artist – and so the network machines continues to churn. When I quizzed Shapiro about his experiences with celebrity he professed similar sentiments:

ATJ: Finally, from your own experience, how powerful is the role of 'celebrity' in these social networks in obtaining friends/followers?

Do you agree that, in the context of online social networks, celebrity can create celebrity?

JSS: There's no question that celebrity creates celebrity. You know what they say – it's all about who you know. People always assume if you know important people then you're important as well. That's not true of course, but as I said in my Journal piece, lots of people on Facebook probably think I'm a pretty important guy – I figure what they don't know won't hurt them.'

In the environment of social networks, a multifaceted idea of celebrity exists. In this space there are offline celebrities for whom this arena is an important place to interact with their fan-base; however, the numerous possibilities and massive audience of these networks has also given rise to the net-celebrity. The net-celebrity can be self-made or celebrity-created, talented or talentless, a social climber or a social fraudster. This celebrity is as famous as their friend/follower count and/or hits on their page. The paparazzi and the fans are one and the same. They share, re-tweet, copy and paste links and files of the net-celebrity's blogs, photographs, music and posts. The net-celebrity may be recognised offline, but their celebrity status has been made, maintained and remains online. Much of this fame is created in networks such as *YouTube*, but it is in the post/blogs and tweets of the social networks where this information moves and the celebrity status grows. Although celebrities whose status has been created offline use these sites as another mechanism to maintain fans, it is not their only fan base. For net-celebrities, these websites maintain them, but if the celebrity does not engage with the people who made them, the fans will be quick to take their status away. These are, however, real celebrities that exist in a real space, with a real fan base. Like reality television, online social networks have provided an arena for a new form of celebrity to exist. Net-celebrities highlight how everyday use of social networks can quickly evolve into something new. Users are performers of the everyday. In relation to the actor, Simmel writes:

> The actor raises *all* the visual and acoustical elements of reality into a perfectly framed unity. This is accomplished through the balance of style, the logic of rhythm, the movement of moods, the recognizable relationship between character and action, and through the subordination of all details under the apex of the whole. The actor thus stylizes all sensual phenomena into unity.[46]

In the evolution of the net-celebrity, digital cameras, video cameras, software and text have allowed social network users to stylise and act out their own personally scripted everyday reality. Living life through the screen does, as Benjamin suggests, mediate the user's performance.[48] However, in doing so it allows them a certain freedom to perform aspects of their lives as they wish others to see them – this relates to all users, not just net-celebrities. Unlike reality television, the actions of the performers come before the fame. Whether what they did was good or bad does not matter. The important part is that someone viewed it and enjoyed it enough to click 'follow'.

Celebrities both participate and create celebrity in social networks and their involvement in these networks is revealing. Celebrities participate in different ways depending on the network. The way in which they participate on *twitter* is particularly thought-provoking as it reveals how boundaries for contact between celebrities and the public are being reformulated. Celebrity participation in networks highlights the manifestation and impact of fraudulent accounts on a celebrity's digital presence, as well as other aspects of their life, which in turn means that these accounts need to be monitored. Social networks are a place for celebrity creation and celebrity participation. Celebrity creation on these websites differs between networks, but can be loosely described as those made famous by friend count or those made famous by talent. Networks can maintain a fan base for celebrities (those who are famous or rising to fame) or create the net-celebrity. Net-celebrity status is either fleeting or is contained entirely within the Internet. Net-celebrities are famous as a result of their digital presence. The evolution of this presence either sustains or destroys the net-celebrity's status. Transient or not, the net-celebrity is real. Celebrity participation and creation discloses the importance of the digital presence. In terms of participation this presence can impact on the life of the celebrity both on- and offline. In terms of celebrity creation the digital presence plays a starring role, and as with participation, the digital presence can help to create a fanbase and build the celebrity status. The development of the user's presence can also create a net-celebrity, possibly explaining why it is difficult for net-celebrities to transfer their success to an offline environment. How a celebrity acts in, or is created by, a network impacts on their own life and the lives of their fans. Whether it is for fame or fandom, participation or creation, positive or negative publicity, the existence of 'celebrity' in these networks is representative of the varied and complex ways that the digital presence intersects with users' lives.

Notes

1. I checked the validity of this message through this official website and *Valebrity* (an Internet resource that validates celebrity social networking accounts).
2. A dream that became a reality when I received a reply to a tweet from Russell Brand.
3. After the completion of this book, I discovered that Noel Fielding's *Facebook* account is actually fraudulent.
4. Nayor, P.K. (2009) *Seeing Stars*. New Delhi: Sage Publications, p. 114.
5. Lily Allen and Trent Reznor are considered to be Internet pioneers for releasing their albums online.
6. Puente, M. (2009) 'Relationships in a twist over Twitter'(Life), in *USA Today*, 15 April, p. 01D.
7. *Ibid*; Coyle, C. (2009) 'Networking sets Ireland a Twitter', *Sunday Times*, 15 February, p. 3; Freydkin, D. (2009) 'All a-Twitter with Technology', *USA Today*, 27 March, p. 13D.
8. Puente, *op. cit.*
9. Friedman E. & Marikar, S. (2009) 'Did Moore's Twitter Feed Stop a Suicide?', available at: *http://abcnews.go.com/Entertainment/AheadoftheCurve/story?id=7248406&page=1* (accessed 7 May 2009).
10. Lee, S. & Scott, D. (2009) 'The process of celebrity fan's constraint negotiation', *Journal of Leisure Research*, 41(2): 140.
11. Notable, well followed, phweeters (phony tweeters) include: director Michael Bay (@michael_bay), actor William Shatner (@WilliamShatner2), *24* character Jack Bauer (@jackbauer) and *Star Wars* character Darth Vader (@DarthVader). Paul, I. (2009) '15 Fake and Funny Twitter Accounts', available at: *http://www.pcworld.com/article/159492/15_fake_and_funny_twitter_accounts.html* (accessed 11 May 2009).
12. Coyle, *op. cit.*
13. Valebrity available at: *http://valebrity.com/*.
14. *Facebook*, *MySpace* and *twitter* all have 'Terms of Service' which clearly state that users are not to provide any false or misleading information. Breech of these conditions can result in deletion of material or suspension of accounts. All three networks, however, state that they are not responsible for the types of material distributed.
15. Saurine, A. (2008) 'Stephanie Rice Facebook pictures censored', available at: *http://www.news.com.au/dailytelegraph/story/0,22049,23468911-5001021,00.html*, (accessed 12 January 2009).
16. Freykdin, *op. cit.*
17. Showbuzz (2009) 'Ashton Kutcher', available at: *http://www.news.com.au/entertainment/celebrity/showbuzz/index/0,26286,5038162-5010840-6,00.htm* (accessed 14 April 2009).
18. Nayor, *op. cit.*, p. 114.
19. Showbuzz (2009) 'Russell Brand' available at: *http://www.news.com.au/entertainment/celebrity/showbuzz/index/0,26286,5038446-5010840-8,00.html* (accessed 14 April 2009).
20. Twitter (2009) 'TalesOfWhim' available at: *https://twitter.com/TalesofWhim* (accessed 14 April 2009).

21. I emailed news.com.au about their use of *twitter* comments as direct quotes and omitting a context, but did not receive a reply.

22. News.com.au is one of the largest online news network in Australia. 'The site has access to Australia's largest news gathering network, with News Limited's 3000 journalists, more than 100 newspapers, three wire services and a dedicated team of online reporters contributing reports.' News.com.au, 'Our Content', available at: *http://www.news.com.au/help* (accessed 10 June 2009).

23. Splash News (2009) 'Chris Brown speaks out on Facebook', available at: *http://www.nypost.com/p/news/national/item_2oAxyPk0GgxqQjBgyR4V3L* (accessed 10 June 2009).

24. Reuters (2009) 'Chris Brown sorry and seeking counselling', available at: *http://www.abc.net.au/news/stories/2009/02/16/2492124.htm* (accessed 10 June 2009).

25. James, O. (2007) *Affluenza*. Reading: Vermillon, p. 43.

26. James focuses on Australia, New Zealand, Britain and America.

27. James *op. cit.*, p. vi.

28. Robin, M. (1995) 'Cyber space and the world we live in'. *Cyberspace/Cyberbodies/Cyberpunk*. London: Sage Publications, p. 139.

29. DC Shoe co-founder, turned rally driver, Kenny Block is a good example of how a viral message can influence a user's life. The viral messages of Block's rally driving developed his status as a net-celebrity and highlighted him as one the world's best rally drivers.

30. Shapiro, J.S. (2009) 'Confessions of a Facebook social climber', available at: *http://online.wsj.com/article/SB123569857063289235.html* (accessed 13 March 2009).

31. Worthington, C. (2009) available at: *http://coreyworthington.org* (accessed 11 January 2009).

32. A comparison between the Anscomb and Worthington parties was actually conducted by Australian gossip and pop culture website Defamer (2008) available at: *http://www.defamer.com.au/tags/gemma-anscomb/* (accessed 11 January 2009) as well as cited in a profile set-up on Wordpress (2008) available at: *http://en.wordpress.com/tag/gemma-anscomb/* (accessed 11 January 2009).

33. Bracchi, P. (2008) 'The world of real party animals: the internet gatecrashers who drug dogs, have group sex and trash homes' available at: *http://www.dailymail.co.uk/news/article-528593/The-world-real-party-animals--The-internet-gatecrashers-drug-dogs-group-sex-trash-homes.html* (accessed 22 February 2009).

34. News.com.au (2009) 'Party pest Corey Worthington passes up Zoo Weekly job', *http://www.news.com.au/entertainment/story/0,28383,25618884-5013560,00.html* (accessed 11 June 2009).

35. Adalian, J. (2007) 'Britney guy may get TV gig', available at: *http://www.variety.com/article/VR1117972243.html?categoryid=14&cs=1* (accessed 11 March 2009).

36. Crocker, C. (2009) 'Chris Crocker's TV show?', available at: *http://www.youtube.com/watch?v=p48f0ZLQn9w* (accessed 11 March 2009).

37. Plagenoef, S. (2006) 'Lily Allen', available at: *http://pitchfork.com/features/interviews/6476-lily-allen/* (accessed 13 March 2009).

38. Weiner, J. (2006) 'Tila Tequila for President', available at: *http://www.slate.com/id/2139691/* (accessed 13 March 2009).
39. Press Release 'More than half of MySpace visitors are now age 35 or older, as the site's demographic composition continues to shift', available at: *http://www.comscore.com/Press_Events/Press_Releases/2006/10/More_than_Half_MySpace_Visitors_Age_35* (accessed 13 March 2009).
40. *RollingStone* (2009) 'Arctic Monkeys biography', available at: *http://www.rollingstone.com/artists/arcticmonkeys/biography* (accessed 13 March 2009).
41. *Ibid.*
42. Binelli, M. (2006) 'Artists to watch: U.K rock kings Arctic Monkeys', *http://www.rollingstone.com/artists/arcticmonkeys/articles/story/9447897/uk_rock_kings_arctic_monkeys* (accessed 13 March 2009).
43. *Prefixmag* (2009) 'Arctic Monkeys aren't fooling around (part 1)', available at: *http://www.prefixmag.com/features/arctic-monkeys/arent-fooling-around-part-1-of-2/12565/* (accessed 14 March 2009).
44. Grossman, L. (2006) 'Tila Tequila', available at: *http://www.time.com/time/magazine/article/0,9171,1570728,00.html* (accessed 14 March 2009).
45. Fallon, J. (2009) *The Jimmy Fallon Show.* New York: NBC.
46. Simmel, G. (1968) (trans) K. Peter Etztkorn. *The Conflict in Modern Culture and Other Essays.* New York: Teachers College Press, p. 92.
47. Arctic Monkeys (2005) 'I Bet You Look Good On The Dancefloor', *Whatever People Say I am That's What I'm Not.* London: Domino Records.
48. Benjamin, W. (2008) *The Work of Art in the Age of Mechanical Reproduction.* London: Penguin Books, pp. 17–18.

4

Putting the social in social networks

There are many different forms of socialising that can be undertaken within social networks. In this chapter I investigate varied types of interactions to demonstrate how the social informs, and is informed by, the user's digital presence. This is to reaffirm the assertion that a digital presence is inextricably linked to a user's real life. I outline the numerous types of socialising that occur in networks, for example friendship, profile building, dating and gaming. In Chapter two I identified the different 'features' that each network offers. Following on from this, I approach how different network features stimulate social interaction. Textual communication, photographs and videos, as well as groups and fan pages, are components that demonstrate how information shared within the network(s) shapes those networks and encourages socialising. The interaction of the user with the network expands their digital presence. Information that is communicated through a profile remains online, even when the user is not, which leads into a discussion of how socialising in networks transforms a user's digital presence and affects a user's life in both positive and negative ways.

Friends or followers are important aspects of the social network machine. If users do not interact with other profiles then the social label of these networks is superfluous. Similarly to my earlier examination of celebrity participation within networks, friends can be marker of popularity or fame. The 'friending' of others helps the user to create a network with which they share information and their life. *MySpace* and *Facebook* both use the label of 'friends' to define other users who have either added the user to, or been allowed to view, their profile. The ability to 'friend' or follow someone differs depending on the network and whether the profile is public or private. Friendship, in a social network, is a loose description that covers family, colleagues, friends, acquaintances and those who a user has met online. Due to the spectrum of friend types in networks, profile accessibility (private or public) and privacy settings are of premium importance. In later chapters I look at the digital presence and specific issues relating to workplaces, cyber-bullying and harassment. In the later section of this chapter I discuss how the digital presence can be a negative influence on a user's life, but I largely focus here on the positive aspects of socialising and building a digital presence in the social network machine.

Profile building shapes a user's digital presence and enables them to socialise. In Chapter two I identified that it is the 'About Me' information that is disclosed that creates an identity and it is this, plus the actions of the user, that shapes the digital presence. The actions undertaken by the user build up their profile. I define profile building as any information on the social network that is connected to the user's profile. Information is shared for both socialising purposes. The amount of information added to a profile helps the user to show snippets of their life, from the party they went to at the weekend, to a video of their child's dance recital or just to share what they had for breakfast. All this information may be very interesting, but no more than a diary with pictures unless there is someone to share with it. Lacy writes:

> When done well, social networking, media and user-generated content sites tap into – and exploit – core human emotions. Blogs, and sites such as YouTube, Yelp, Revision3 and Digg are ostensibly about getting the entertainment and news that you want. But it's the stroking of your ego that makes them so powerful. Having thousands of people read your opinion on something or your minute-to-minute life story … But more important than entertainment, self-expression, or ego boosting is the human need to connect.[1]

Lacy highlights that friends are an important element of social networking. Although this might be obvious given the type of network, I am curious as to why people need to share huge amounts of information with people that they barely know. I would not start showing a primary school acquaintance pictures of my birthday party if I bumped into them on the street, but I allow them to see them on *Facebook* because this is in the name of socialising.

It is important to reflect on why a user adds friends in such a haphazard manner. Personally, I feel it is nice to log into a network and see a large number of people who (seem to) have some interest in your life. However, I also believe that users still view the screen as a barrier between the on- and offline world, and that the information uploaded and interacted with in a network exists in a cyber-bubble. In this way such networks are like a leisure centre, somewhere you can go every day and hang out with your 'friends'. With regard to Lefebvre's idea of leisure, Highmore writes: 'for Lefebvre, leisure in the "modern world" is a routinized instance of a capitalist everyday life, as well as evidence of the continuation of festival'.[2] The 'continuation of festival' is recognised in the excessive use of social networks in various areas of our lives. Lefebvre suggests that 'everyday life is made of recurrences: gestures of labour and leisure, mechanical movements both human and properly mechanic, hours, days, weeks, months, years, linear and cyclical repetitions, natural and rational time'.[3] Social networks, as discussed in later chapters, blur the boundaries between labour and leisure. Highmore refers to Lefebvre's example of the camping holiday to show 'the interaction of work and the negation of work'[4], where 'work and leisure are barely distinguishable, and everyday life in its entirety becomes play'.[5] Leisure activities are conducted in social networks. When combined with the digital technology that allows instant access to these networks, this constant ability to socialise and undertake leisure means that other traditionally non-leisure activities in a user's life – work for example – are now being affected. It is the social side of these networks that gives users a buzz, and can make a user feel good about having a 'social' life when their life offline might not allow for one.

Socialising on these networks occurs in different ways and textual communication is a large part of this. The main catalysts for textual communication are: tweets on *twitter*, status updates and wall posts on *Facebook*, and status, mood updates and blogs on *MySpace*. Returning to my earlier analogy, that users are the lifeblood of the network, status updates are the mechanism by which it is circulated. They allow a profile to live, which in turn allows the social network to function. Tweets feed *twitter*, and without interesting microblogs and bloggers *twitter* would cease to be of interest. Socialising in this network is undertaken in a voyeuristic and non-engaging manner. The *twitter* user is privy to the 'behind the screen' goings-on of the people they are following. They can read about their lives and if they feel that they need to respond, then a quick tweet can be issued. The constant updates allow users to dwell on the fringe of celebrities or other users' lives. They can have these instant text messages delivered to their phones, computers or both and just read, as if they were meant solely for them. A high degree of digital connectivity allows the user constant access to the Internet.

By the time Web 2.0 came around, the Internet was no longer its own distinct land. It was woven into people's everyday lives. This was partially due to the advances in networking and computer technology. As high-speed connections, wireless Internet routers, WiFi-enabled laptops, and Web-enabled cell phones became more common, people could be online instantly and anywhere not just at a desk.[6]

Connecting to networks like *twitter* is like living in the city, but never walking the streets. A user can be content just knowing that there is a social buzz going on around them. Status updates help to keep the network churning and the lines of communication between users open. The current, constant and often instant nature of posts and replies stimulate conversations and draw disparate friend groups together. The everyday dispersal of comedic quips, friendly banter, advice and well wishes, although often glaringly superficial, seem to provide the user with a caring network. This connection, as Lacy asserts, 'is a far more powerful use of the Web than for something like buying a book online'.[7] *MySpace* offers the ability to communicate in a similar manner to *Facebook*, although the format of these functions encourages the user to pontificate rather than to socialise. Although repartee between users can be instigated, the main focus of the network is profile building. This network is primarily focused on the popular cultural tastes of the user, which flows in to how they communicate and socialise on the network, rather than on multifaceted socialising.

Flickr is a social network that is based on communicating through photographs and video. Users can upload their photographs to the website and friends or other site users can view and comment on them. Its main point is to share and stimulate conversation based on these images. *Flickr*, however, is not the only social network that relies on photographs as a way to communicate and stimulate socialising. They are a pivotal part of other social networks such as *twitter*, *MySpace* and *Facebook*, as they first and foremost show current and potential friends or followers *who* the user is. The photograph not only helps to build the user's profile and adds to their digital presence, but it can add to the digital presence of other users in these networks. As a result, choosing which snapshots to upload is of some importance.

The proclamation that photographs are a form of communication and socialising might seem to be an obvious one, a fait accompli. However, the reasons why this type of information is so necessary, and undertaken with such vigour within these networks, is an intrinsic part of this discussion. In *Camera Lucida* Barthes observes that:

> ... a photograph can be the object of three practices (or of three emotions, or of three intentions): to do, to undergo, to look. The

Operator is the Photographer. The *Spectator* is ourselves, all of us who glance through collections of photographs – in magazines and newspapers, in books, albums, archives … And the person or thing photographed is the target, the referent, a kind of little simulacrum, any *eidolon* emitted by the object, which I should like to call the *Spectrum* of the Photograph, because this word, retains, through its root, a relation to 'spectacle'.[8]

Within social networks Barthes three intentions come together as one in the form of the user's profile picture. The profile picture is the first image that a user sees when clicking on their own, or another user's, profile. It is also an image that, with access to digital technology such as camera phones, webcams and inbuilt laptop cameras, is often taken by the user. This results in the user being simultaneously the operator, spectator and spectrum. The photograph or picture that is uploaded is purposefully formed to project a certain image of the user. Robbins remarks on the purpose of Barthes' work:

Cognition is experienced here as a complex process, mediated through the body and suffused with affect and emotion … Barthes project is to explore the experience of photography … For Barthes, understanding the representational nature of these images cannot be separated from understanding the sensations – the touch – of desire or of grief that they provoke.[9]

The nature of the profile picture is to display an image that represents the user, which in turns adds to, and shapes, the digital presence. The range of these pictures – from no picture to glamour shots – is in itself intriguing. From personal experience the main shots portray how the user is feeling at that particular time in their life. So they are there to 'provoke' feelings of celebrations, encouragement or grief and condolences. Benjamin writes, 'in the transient expression of a human countenance in early photographs, we catch one final glimpse of aura'.[10] This can be seen in the images that are chosen as the profile picture. For example, if the user has just been married then a romantic wedding shot is often used on a profile, if they are in a band then a band or gig shot will be used and if they have had a baby then the baby is often the profile shot. Slater writes, 'there is pressure for photography to structure everyday life in the very process of representing it'.[11] These photographs are not only uploaded to illustrate the current state of the user's life, but also to stimulate conversations about the spectrum. How these profile pictures are used differs in the various networks.

On *Facebook* a user can have a history of their profile shots, which not only illustrates the user's digital presence, but can be reused as the current profile picture whenever they desire. 'Electronic images are frozen, do not fade; their quality is not elegiac, they are not just registrations of mortality. Digital techniques produce images in cryogenised form: they can be awoken, re-animated, brought "up to date".'[12] *MySpace* allows the user to pick a profile shot from one of their albums and demonstrates Robbins' principle. As a user and as a spectator in multiple social networks, it would seem that users 'fall back' on these images when current photographs do not adequately portray how they want to view themselves. For example, I returned to a pre-pregnancy profile picture when I was eight months pregnant, as I did not want my chubby face to represent me or be a point for discussion. The knowledge that a profile picture is not only portraying the user, but can also be a point of discussion, means that the photograph plays an important role in socialising on networks. *Twitter* only allows one shot to remain on the website at one time. Unlike with *Facebook* or *MySpace* the user must replace their profile picture rather than switch between images already on the network. There are also no photo 'albums' on *twitter* so there really is only one photo to say it all. Barthes writes:

> Since the Photograph is pure contingency and can be nothing else (it is always *something* that is represented) – contrary to the text which, by the sudden action of a single word, can shift a sentence from description to reflection – it immediately yields up those 'details' which constitute the very raw material of ethnological knowledge.[13]

Barthes' idea resonates when put in the context of *twitter*, where the single profile picture is something that, as with other networks, captures the image of the user, but it is the *words* of the user that shift how the user is actually read. Photographs frame not only the way in which a user views themselves, but also how others perceive them. Photographs also stimulate socialising in a number of ways.

Prior to examining why photographs are a pivotal tool for socialising, the way in which they are presented in these networks needs to be outlined. The prominence of photographs and albums differs on each network. As previously stated, only one photograph is permitted to be displayed as the profile picture on *twitter*, although the user can link to their photographs using *twitpics*. This system of having to click through links to another service means that the tweet that leads to the link must be enticing. In *Image–Music–Text*, Barthes comments on the press photograph and suggests that:

> even from the perspective of a purely immanent analysis, the structure of the photograph is not an isolated structure; it is in communication with at least one other structure namely the text – title, caption or article – accompanying every press photograph.[14]

This can be applied to the textual communication that accompanies photographs in all networks, but in the structure of *twitter* it holds a particular resonance. Communication relating to the photograph is usually enacted on *twitpics* itself, rather than on *twitter*. The lack of photographs on the website keeps the focus on microblogging as the main form of communication. On *MySpace* and *Facebook* photographs form a larger part of networking. A user on *MySpace* can have several albums that are found by clicking on the user's profile picture. By contrast, on *Facebook*, the photo albums are not hidden and are visible directly on the user's profile. The continual updating and creation of albums help these networks to live.

Photographs work as a tool for socialising in a number of ways. First, the photographs themselves often portray 'socialising'. Birthdays, parties, weddings, travelling and many other events are captured on camera and uploaded to the website. Through photography, social networks publicise the private by uploading snapshots of the user's social life. Slater writes:

> Photography is intimately bound up with domesticity and the private world, and has been since its inception. This is evident in family photographs – portraits and snapshots, images of familial rites of passage such as weddings – in which the seemingly existential relation between photographs and memory folds individual and collective identities into familial narrative time.[15]

The element of the social circle, or what Slater refers to as the 'individual and collective identities',[16] within uploaded photographs is not only an image of offline socialising, but is an instigator of network communication within. The 'tag' function plays an importation role in this relationship. This tool requires the user to click on individual people in the photograph and label their presence. It is available in both *Facebook* and *MySpace* and enables the user to notify their friends (and friends of friends) of their appearance within the images. The tagging function (depending on the privacy settings) can allow the user in the picture, as well as their friends within the networks, to see these pictures. The tag function gives the user the ability to digitally mark another user. Therefore, the power of the photograph in these networks is considerable and although sometimes the attention of these pictures might be unwanted, the ability to share them with a large number of friends marks them as a positive element of the networks.

Photography is considered a leisure activity[17] and social networks (especially those like *Flickr*) allow users to share their creative endeavours with their 'friends'. The presence of photographs allows the 'network' to comment, encourage or critique the user's photographic hobby or career. Although still in the category of leisure, photographing 'things' extends beyond the art itself. Users in a network may also take images of other creative hobbies or create an album to track a long-term project such as a house or car being built. The user can share information or gain advice from a wide range of 'friends'. These images become sites of socialising because once they exist within the network they are not simply images of things; the comments from both the user and their friends provide them with context, history and aesthetic importance. In Chapter three I briefly noted the problems of context with regard to status updates. Here we can see how when other users comment on contents such as photographs they give this element a context and history.[18] Simmel writes:

> Even the lowest, intrinsically ugly phenomenon can be dissolved into context of color and form, feeling and experience which provide it with significance. To involve ourselves deeply and lovingly with the even most common product, which, would be banal and repulsive in its isolated experience, enables us to conceive of it, too, as a ray and image of the final unity of all things from which beauty and meaning flow. Every philosophical system, every religion, every moment of our heightened emotional experience searches for symbols which are appropriate to their expression. If we pursue this possibility of aesthetic appreciation to its final point, we find that there are no essential differences amongst things. Our world view turns to aesthetic pantheism. Every point contains within itself the potential of being redeemed to absolute aesthetic importance. To the adequately trained eye the totality of beauty, the complete meaning of the world as a whole, radiates from every single point.[19]

Photographs might be contingent, but the context, comments and connections help them to live. Photographs are aesthetic shards of the everyday and users take joy and pain from engaging with them.

Photographs in social networks play a positive role in the lives of users because they allow users to upload and share parts of their life with many people who might not ordinarily share in it. The act of uploading the photographs is in itself a form of communication. Even if other users do not respond, the act of sharing photographic information (which often includes other users) is a way of including others in the user's life. Through content, tagging and commenting, photographs encourage users to communicate and socialize with each other. So 'socialising' in a network can help build a user an online social circle when they might not currently have one 'offline'. Networks such as *Facebook* and *MySpace* can provide significant relief for those users who are permanently or temporarily isolated from family or friends. The sharing of images demonstrates the positive impact that having a digital presence has on a user's life. The positive influence is demonstrated through the conversations that images instigate, as photographs play a significant role in social connection. Barthes remarks:

> Show your photographs to someone – he will immediately show you his: 'Look this is my brother; this is my child,' etc.; the Photograph is never anything but antiphon of 'Look," "See," "Here it is"; it points a finger at certain *vis-à-vis*, and cannot escape deictic language.[20]

Barthes is correct in that a photograph encourages a certain amount of deictic language, but although this language is seen in the uploading of photographs, the engagement with photographs by other users goes beyond this surface level connection. In part I would suggest that this has something to do with a user choosing to view the photographs rather than being overtly shown them. *Facebook* is a one-stop shop for the isolated user or traveller to share their photographs and videos with multiple friends, as well as chat or email.

Like photographs, videos also play a unique role in social networks. They are a tool to share 'private' information such as video messages of holidays, weddings or sharing the first steps of a child. In this way, like photographs, they are examples of socialising, because they contain social activities and also instigate communication within the networks. *Facebook* and *MySpace* allow a user to record directly from a webcam, upload from a computer drive or link to a video. Similar to *twitpic* there are services such as *TwitVid* and *Twiddeo* that allow *twitter* users to share videos. Videos give life-like qualities – a body and a voice – to the users on the networks. Benjamin suggests:

> Just as lithography virtually implied the illustrated newspaper, so did photography foreshadow the sound film, [because,] Since the eye perceives more swiftly than the hand can draw, the process of pictorial reproduction was accelerated so enormously that it could keep pace with speech.[21]

Users can see, hear and watch their friends and family at events that they were or were not at. So these texts add another dimension to the network, providing positive experiences and an avenue to share and receive information.

Videos, and photographs to a similar extent, are also used to share public information. Usually achieved through linking, users can share videos from networks such as *YouTube* within social networks. Video types including music clips, comedy sketches, short films and movie trailers can be shared and commented on within the network. Similar to private videos, public videos are shared with the intention of social commentary. Debates between the user, friends, acquaintances and unknowns can all be instigated by one simple link. (Re)New(ed) friendships and alliances can be sparked through the shared fandom or hatred of an uploaded video. The sharing of videos links the user to other cultures and subcultures. Video sharing can spark both textual comments and video responses, with a chain of visual fodder for the user's network of friends to devour, share, relish and spit out. One place where the sharing of 'public' video and photographs is most prominent is on the group and fan pages within the social networks.

Group and fan pages help to stoke the fires of popularity for networks such as *MySpace*. It is interesting to note how *MySpace* general profiles are set out like those group pages for bands and music acts, whereas *Facebook* has just changed its group and fan pages to look more like user profile pages. I suggest this has something to do with *MySpace* users having some desire to be rockstars, whereas *Facebook* seems to see a certain sense in making celebrities look like regular users. This change is quite twitteresque and *Facebook* seems to be riding on the shirt-tails of this popular format. *Twitter* does not have group or fan pages, and as mentioned in previous chapters, the user simply 'follows' the actual celebrity. Fan and group pages are prominent within social networks because they are a place where fans do not just follow the lives of their heroes and idols, but also interact with those who share similar interests. In this regard, Jenkins asserts:

> Like cultural scavengers, fans reclaim works that others regard as 'worthless' trash, finding a source of popular capital. Like rebellious

children, fans refuse to read by the rules imposed upon them by the schoolmasters. For the fan, reading becomes a kind of play, responsive only to its own loosely structured rules and generating its own kinds of pleasure.[22]

Through the uploading of 'public' videos and photographs to user profiles and fan and group pages, the fan can fit the celebrity/character/thing into their own lives. On *Facebook* there is a distinction between the fan and group pages. This is mainly in terms of structure rather than the 'thing' itself. By this I mean that fan pages are not just simply created for celebrity, but can be for anything that is popular such as a character, food, car or sport. The difference in the structure is that 'fan' pages, as opposed to group pages, have a main wall for the subject of fandom, and a wall that is 'just for fans'. Fans can 'comment' on information posted on the main wall, but can only write freely in the 'just for fans' section. Fans, however, can upload videos and photographs to fan pages and this is where they (re)claim the object of their fandom. Videos of the fans meeting their idols and short films are uploaded, shared with and commented on by other fans. Users can also join, be invited to or create groups for 'things' that they are a fan of. For example, the 'Salty Plum Appreciation Group' is an open group, which is 'a hat tip to those of us who love the Salty Plum (also known as Salted Plums, Salted Prunes or Dried Plums)'.[23] Fan and group pages are not just there to show a user's allegiance to musicians and dried fruit. Fandom is a leisure activity, and fan pages within social networks are another aspect of socialising and leisure. Jenkins states:

> For some women, trapped in low-paying jobs or within the socially isolated sphere of the housewife, participation within an (inter)national network of fans grants a degree of dignity and respect otherwise lacking. For others, fandom offers a training ground for the development of professional skills and an outlet for creative impulses constrained by their workday lives.[24]

Jenkins assertion regarding fans fits into my debate regarding both fan and group pages, as well as the networks themselves. Fan pages on these websites provide another avenue for participation and distraction from isolation. They provide a space for like-minded users to converse with each other and, depending on the network, the idol/celebrity/character in question.

In Chapter three I articulated the role of celebrity within social networks in terms of how a digital presence, which is largely shaped by interaction with fans, affects their life. The user's digital presence enables fans to engage with celebrities and fan pages, which in turn shapes their life. Grossberg argues that:

> The relations between culture and audiences cannot be understood simply as the process by which people appropriate already existing texts into the already constituted context of their social position, their experience or needs. Nor can it be described in terms which suggest that the audience is simply passive acceding to the predetermined nature of the text. In fact, both audiences and texts are continuously remade – their identity and effectiveness reconstructed – by relocating their place within different contexts. The audience is always caught up in the continuous reconstruction of cultural contexts which enable them to consume, interpret and use texts in specific ways.[25]

The relationship between fans and celebrities demonstrates Grossberg's argument. In fact, the relationship between a user's digital presence, their friends and followers is an apt example of how texts are remade and reconstructed. Fan pages also allow the user to create photographs and videos that reflect on, and engage with, their fandom. This is another example of how a digital presence can be a positive value adding experience in a user's life. Fan pages are also spaces located within a social network, and are popular cultural sites that users can also become 'fans' of. Each network has legions of fans and social network haters. They share their love/hate relationships, articulated through the network itself, other Internet networks and forums, as well as via merchandise such as t-shirts, mouse pads and mugs.

Each social network is purpose built for a certain kind of socialising. *Twitter* is focused on communicating and socialising around the everyday activities in users' lives through the art of microblogging. *MySpace* is focused on shared popular cultural interests with a specific focus on music. Musicians' pages, videos, photographs, blogs and chat allow the users to socialise in various ways around this material. *Facebook* draws in multiple aspects of socialising and communicating, creating a one-stop shop for social interaction. It allows users to chat in real time, share information and engage with multiple online activities through the use of applications such as chat, dating and games all in the one network. *Facebook* has placed a multitude of online activities that require social interaction in one space, creating what amounts to an online leisure centre. Users can be socialising in multiple ways at the same time. For example, I can be playing games such as *Scrabulous* and communicating with friends in-game, while simultaneously using the network's chat function outside of the game to talk to other users. The chat function is a seemingly positive aspect of the network as it allows the user to converse in real time. It is also another element of the network's lifeblood. The fact that conversations are real time, and private, gives the network a greater feel of social engagement. The chat function is also an undercurrent, something I discuss in subsequent chapters. Through chat, updates to the user's profile page, group associations, quizzes and applications, *Facebook* encourages a high level of social engagement with the network itself. The one element that all of these websites have in common is the sharing of information. It is this sharing that underpins all social aspects of the networks and is what allows them to 'live'.

Each user, to some degree, controls the amount and type of information that is shared within the network(s). There must always be some intention behind the information that is communicated, because a user's existence in an online social network indicates a desire to socialise, or at the very least to put forth an online social presence. Therefore, the information that is uploaded is there to be shared. Social networks now form a significant part of users' social lives, either by giving the user a social circle where they otherwise would not have one, expanding on their existing social circle, or creating an exclusively online social circle. I mentioned previously that each network is purpose-built for different types of socialising, and therefore different types of information are shared. The reason why users participate in multiple networks is to fulfil different aspects of their 'social lives'. I use *Facebook*, for example, to keep in touch with my close and extended groups of friends and family. I use *MySpace*'s blog function, listen to music and read about the latest music releases. I use *twitter* to follow celebrities I am a fan of and to microblog to followers, the majority of whom I do not know outside of the network. I consciously interact differently on the networks not only because of their different structures and content, but because of the different kinds of 'friends' I have on each. I find a freedom in the lack of personal information available on my *twitter* profile. I have one photograph, a three-word biography and a link to a website containing my written publications. I share short tweets about things that I find interesting or funny, to people I do not know. I do this for the same reason that other people on *twitter* have public profiles, because I want people to find me interesting. The information that I share, often in the form of 'rants', is carefully constructed. I do not know the majority of my followers and I want to make tweets as amusing as possible. It is almost a virtual comedy gig where I can monitor and delete posts that are not funny or, in order to impress fellow writers, are not grammatically correct. I use my digital presence to make me feel good or keep me entertained. My life is influenced not only by sharing information but also by the information that I read from other users.

On *Facebook* I share information in a rather haphazard manner. I upload random photographs of people, events and objects that interest me. I update my status regularly with quotes, lyrics, how I am feeling or what I am doing. For me *Facebook* is a more personal experience, which is odd given the number of friends that I have and the level to which I actually 'know' them. It is an extension of my 'offline' social network and I use it as a base for socialising. I can share information and interact with my friends and family who are overseas. The relationship with my friends on *Facebook* is two-way. Unlike *twitter* I am not posting to an unknown audience. I know these people, I know that they will respond and so I pump information into the network to build my profile, instigate responses and network socially. I would not call *twitter* a passive network because there is definitely a freedom to be able to rant to no one in particular, and I believe that *twitter* is largely about reading, following and engaging (even if that engagement is in the form lurking) with people of interest. *Facebook* is probably the locus of my digital presence because it is the network where my 'friends' actually 'know' me. I receive more 'social' value from it because I add more information to the network and engage in multilayered forms of communication.

MySpace is directed at a very specific audience and encourages a certain type of information to be shared. It is less about the sharing of bulk information about the user's life and is more focused on the user's leisure – namely popular cultural – interests. The network, although offering applications and services that are similar to those on *Facebook*, really focuses on sharing information on popular cultural interests. However, there are Web 2.0 applications such as *tweetdeck*, *skimmer* and *Eventbox*, which 'mash' the information from various social networks into one application, so the user can update and check a multitude of networks at once. If social media have reached a point where information – for example updates – is being shaped to be appropriate in all networks – so generic updates – then questions as to why a user needs to engage with more than one network need to be pondered.

Although the technologically savvy can use 'mash' up applications to control their generic updates, this does not stop them from using the individual networks as well. So applications such as *tweedeck* can be used to update information that a user wants to share with all of their networks and then the social networks can be updated individually with refined information. Those users heavily involved in social media may very well just use these mash-up applications to control and limit all of their social network updates. However, I believe that the average user tends to operate network-specific applications that are built for devices such as mobile phones – for example *Facebook* or *twitter* applications for the iPhone – to share and control information.

The reason why a user engages in multiple social networks is the same reason that they join just one. As previously articulated, each network is purpose built for a certain type of networking. Users join and use different networks for their different social needs. In the same way that a person has different social circles and different friendships, they also have different online social networks. I use *Facebook* to retain and interact with a large network of friends and I use *twitter* to make new friends, 'meet' new people and see what people are talking/writing about. As a service these networks are constructed so certain amounts of information are easily shared, but it is the users who give the network character and tone. It is the users who, through the sharing of information and interaction, enable the network to grow and evolve. *Twitter*, for example, played an important role in getting out information to organise grassroots protests in Moldova. Natalie Morsar, the alleged 'mastermind' behind the Moldova protests, states:

> It just happened through Twitter, the blogosphere, the internet, SMS, websites and all this stuff. We just met, we brainstormed for 15 minutes, and decided to make a flash mob [internet-organised spontaneous public gathering] ... In several hours, 15,000 people came out into the street.[26]

The power of *twitter* was again witnessed when Iranians used the service to update the world about the protests in Tehran. CNN senior editor Octavia Nasar reported:

> Tweets from 'Change for Iran' were among several that offered real time updates: '... my friend saying more than 100 students arrested, I can't confirm this but the numbers are high. Bastards just attacked us for no reason, I lost count of how much tear gas they launched at us! ... we have now some students with urgent need of medical attention I'm calling out to all ppl who can come here don't leave us.[27]

The power of the people and their tweets in Iran was confirmed when *twitter* rescheduled site maintenance to enable the channels of communication to remain open. The *twitter* blog for 15 June 2009 read:

> A critical network upgrade must be performed to ensure continued operation of Twitter. In coordination with Twitter, our network host had planned this upgrade for tonight. However, our network partners at NTT America recognize the role Twitter is currently playing as an important communication tool in Iran. Tonight's planned maintenance has been rescheduled to tomorrow.[28]

This example of *twitter* being mobilised for grass-roots rebellion is so significant in the context of socialising because it demonstrates the power of sharing information. The use of social networks is often trivialised as technological toys for boring people to tweet/post/update about banal and mundane 'everyday' things such as what they ate for breakfast. Online social networks are more than this. They provide a space for people to come together and socialise, whether that is to give a lonely user the ability to communicate with people, keep a traveller in touch with family or allow a community a way of organising an uprising. There is power in this sharing of everyday information. Each network is a community and within this community there are smaller communities of fans, friends and followers.

The information shared within these communities, through digital presences, has the positive impact of creating and maintaining social circles, which provides users with friendship and the feelings of closeness and well-being. Friends, plus the information shared in a profile – profile building – stimulate socialising. This socialising is what encourages the user to share more information, which in turn builds the profile, shapes the digital presence and helps to develop the social aspect of the network and the friendships made or sustained therein. Developing a digital presence through profile building therefore impacts positively on a user's life by enabling a multitude of social experiences. In the context of this chapter, the information disclosed within the network is being used in a constructive way. This in turn would lead us to the conclusion that the digital presence that is created portrays the user in a positive light. This is something that is not always the case.

Social networking has become embedded in the UK, USA and Australia and the rate of technological development surrounding social networks is increasing. However, due to their relatively short history, the level to which the cultural saturation of social networks (manifested through heightened levels of communication and an abundant amount of information sharing) affects a user's whole life is still unknown. What can be asserted is that there is a clear two-way flow of information between offline facets of the user's life and their digital presence. The types of socialising, via the uploading and interaction of information shared, within the network is representative of this. Profile building adds to the 'action' aspect of the digital presence. Socialising using this digital presence can impact on other areas of the user's life in both positive and negative ways.

As discussed throughout this chapter, socialising online can relieve the frustration of isolation that is felt offline and creating a digital presence is the way that this is achieved. The creation of a digital presence allows the user to build social circles. Engagement with multiple networks allows the user to create multiple circles, which can fulfil their different social needs. Social networks and the digital presence allow a user to feel like they are part of, and engage with, different communities. Developing a digital presence can also lead to an expanded social circle offline. For example, new friendships can be made, or old friendships rekindled, that are based on shared interests discovered through the sharing of information such as popular cultural interests, photographs and links within profiles or through fan pages. There can also be negative consequences of creating a digital presence and engaging with social networks.

For a user who is isolated or lacking in a social circle, networks play an important role in providing a space for him or her to upload, share and communicate different aspects of their life with an expanded network of 'friends'. This constant movement of information is not only what allows these networks to function and expand, but it also shapes and influences the user's digital presence. Although the size and function of the digital presence fills various voids in the lives of the socially isolated, the fact that this information is available to a wide range of people means that it does not operate in a vacuum. Earlier in this chapter I argued that information provided by photographs, videos, status updates and blogs is used to stimulate conversation and these are points for socialising and communal debate. Much positive amusement and social capital can be garnered via social stimulus. However, the two-way flow of information, between the digital presence and the user's on/offline environments, means that the texts and accompanying conversations have a way of leaking into multiple parts of the user's life. The networks contain certain elements that are what I referred to in Chapter three as everyday undercurrents.

A user's life consists of both on- and offline aspects and I believe that the digital presence is the link between these. What happens online does not just stay online. However, because online social networking systems become embedded in 'offline' parts of a user's life (e.g. work, school, university, family and offline recreational or leisure activities) the 'realness' of these networks and the significance of their existence become apparent. Generation Yers are often labelled as technologically savvy, but this alone will only take a user so far when navigating online social networks. The (mis)use of online social networks has the potential to cause users a myriad of problems. Encounters between a user's digital presence and friendships with workmates or employers have resulted in users being reprimanded or fired. Online social networks are also highly visible sites of bullying and harassment. The relationship between workers/users and social networks, and bullying and harassment and social networks, are two distinct areas that are part of our social consciousness. It is for this reason that the second half of this book is dedicated to examining the negative impact of the digital presence on a user's life as well as the demise and finally the death of the digital presence.

This chapter has demonstrated that there are some positive aspects of having a digital presence and participating in social networks. The networks need certain elements in order to function and although each network is built for different types of socialising, there are certain core characteristics that they all have: users, friends and the ability to build, and interact with, a profile. Each network encourages different modes of communication such as textual updates and blogs, as well as the ability to upload photographs and videos. The different networks also have their own form of fan pages. As articulated in this and earlier chapters the user's identity, plus their interactions within the network (linked to profile building), creates their digital presence. A user's digital presence can play a positive role in his or her life in terms of socialising. Social networks provide a space that allows a user to 'socialise' in various capacities. Through their digital presence a user can share different parts of their lives via text, photographs and videos, with a wide 'social' circle. Participating in these networks is a leisure activity and can provide a social space for those who a permanently or temporarily distanced from their offline social circle. The information shared and interacted with within these networks stimulates socialising and in this way online social networks have created microcommunities within a larger community. This is reinforced by the presence of 'applications' such as games as well as fans and group pages. *Facebook* is the most prolific social network in terms of offering a space for multi-level socialising. It provides a one-stop shop for users to get recreational activities, communication and friendship. As a user engages with these varying activities they are adding to their digital presence. In the context of this chapter, the digital presence can be viewed as a positive entity. It is something that allows the user to share parts of their life and engage with different social activities. On a very basic level it is a digital signifier that the user exists, has friends and provides them with a sense of social worth. Much has been, and will be, argued about the negative impacts of social networking and this often hides the reason why these networks were created to begin with – to network socially. As sad as it may sound, these networks can give a life to those who without them would ordinarily feel isolated. They are a space to get a pat on the back or a virtual hug when needed, and for this reason online social networks are not only positive but are also an extraordinarily powerful social tool.

Notes

1. Lacy, S. (2008) *The Stories of Facebook, YouTube and Myspace*. Surrey: Crimson, p. 97.
2. Highmore, B. (2002) *Everyday Life and Cultural Theory*. London: Routledge, p. 129.
3. Lefebvre, H. (1984) *Everyday Life in The Modern World*. S. Rabinovitch (trans.) New Brunswick: Transaction Publishers, p. 18.
4. Highmore, *op. cit.*, p. 128.
5. Lefebvre, H. (1991) *Critique of Everyday Life: Volume 1(1947/1958)*. J. Moore (trans.). London: Verso, p. 33.
6. Lacy, *op. cit.*, pp. 95–6.
7. *Ibid.*, p. 97.
8. Barthes, R. (2000) *Camera Lucida*. London: Vintage Classics, p. 9.
9. Robbins, K. (1994) 'Will image move us still?'. *The Photographic Image in Digital Culture*. London: Routledge, p. 39.
10. Benjamin, W. (2008) *The Work of Art in the Age of Mechanical Reproduction*. London: Penguin Books, p. 14.
11. Slater, D. (1994) 'Domestic photography and digital culture'. *The Photographic Image in Digital Culture*. London: Routledge, p. 130.
12. Robbins, *op. cit.*, p. 41.
13. Barthes, *op. cit.*, p. 28.
14. Barthes, R. (1979) *Image-Music-Text*. Glasgow: Fontana/Collins, p. 16.
15. Slater, *op. cit.*, p. 129.
16. *Ibid.*
17. *Ibid.*, p. 130.
18. However, if a user chooses to monitor (delete, rework, remove) these comments, then the context can become confused. This is something that I explore in Chapter five.

19. Simmel, G. (1968) K. P. Etztkorn (trans). *The Conflict in Modern Culture and Other Essays*. New York: Teachers College Press, p. 69.
20. Barthes (2000) *op. cit.*, p. 5.
21. Benjamin, W. (1973) 'The work of art in the age of mechanical reproduction'. In H. Arendt (ed.) *Illuminations*. Glasgow: Fontana/Collins, p. 221.
22. Jenkins, H. (2006) *Fans, Bloggers and Gamers: Exploring Participatory Culture*. New York: New York University Press, p. 39.
23. Boal, A. (2009) 'Salty Plum Appreciation Group', available at *http://www.facebook.com/home.php#/group.php?gid=6156142619&ref=ts* (accessed 15 March 2009).
24. Jenkins, *op. cit.*, p. 42.
25. Grossberg, L. (1992) 'Is there a fan in the house'. In: L. Lewis (ed.) *The Adoring Audience*. London: Routledge, p. 54.
26. Lungescu, O. (2009) 'Moldova's "Twitter revolutionary" speaks out', available at: *http://news.bbc.co.uk/2/hi/europe/8018017.stm* (accessed 25 April 2009).
27. Nasr, O. (2009) 'Tear gas and Twitter: Iranians take their protests online', available at: *http://edition.cnn.com/2009/WORLD/meast/06/14/iran.protests.twitter/index.html* (accessed 15 June 2009).
28. @Biz (2009) 'Down time rescheduled', available at: *http://blog.twitter.com/2009/06/down-time-rescheduled.html* (accessed 15 June 2009).

5

(Net)Working: online social networks and the New Economy

GOOD JOB'S DON'T FALL FROM THE SKY. NOR, IF THEY DID, WOULD we know what to make of them. Like the aliens who visited us in Cold War science fiction films, they might be regarded as threats to our way of life.[1] – Andrew Ross

The introduction to Andrew Ross's *No-Collar: The Humane Workplace and Its Hidden Costs*[2] presents the reader with the craft and hardship required to obtain a 'good' job. Due to social and economic development, much has changed in terms of what constitutes a job, work, employment or career. Digitised technological advancement and popular culture have moulded ideas of work, workplace structure, professionalism and lifestyle. By approaching theories of Fordism and Post-Fordism, and mapping the spaces and links between the 'New' and 'Old' Economy, the first half of this chapter explores and probes the changes in workplace practices. I explain the different eras and systems of work in order to show how ideas of work have changed, but fragments of these beliefs and structures still inform aspects of contemporary working environments. This discussion is necessary as it provides a context, and history, for current working conditions and ideals. I focus on digitised technological transformations of industry, ideologies of the popular cultural workplace and the how the 'New Economy' has transformed and revealed meanings of work, work ethics and professionalism in Old Economic environments. The use of social networking sites within Old Economic environments is an example of 'New Economic' elements and the second half of this chapter is dedicated to examining the relationship between a user's digital presence and work. The use of networks by employees is a contentious subject and throughout this chapter I identify how their link to the digital presence is challenging contemporary working environments. The issue of the digital presence in the workplace transcends the misuse of social networks by employees. Although the use of networks at work is discussed, it is the interactions with these networks by employees outside of work hours that reveals the importance of the digital presence. In previous chapters I asserted in that the digital presence is always online. By examining the information and actions that are undertaken in social networks, I show how the digital presence can affect a user in the workplace. This reaffirms my assertion that the digital presence is inextricably linked to the real world of the user. As this discussion is framed by the structure of contemporary workplaces, I commence this exploration by looking at the concept of work.

Working nine to five ... what a way to make a living[59]

A conceptualisation of the term 'work' is necessary to initiate any examination into the discourse of work. Paul Ransome suggests four criteria for the basic definition of work:

> Firstly, this definition of work encompasses a number of alternative terms used to denote the performance of an activity. Secondly, this activity is associated with the notion of payment or income. Thirdly, the basic assumption is made that this performance requires the discharge of physical and/or mental energy. Fourthly, there is the expectation that work is in some way useful or expedient, which is to say that working activities can be distinguished from non-working activities such as 'play' or 'leisure', on the grounds that their purpose tends towards some form of quantifiable material gain rather than towards simple enjoyment or relaxation.[3]

'Work' is viewed as an energy-fuelled activity undertaken for gainful purposes. It encompasses such activities as housework, a job or labour. Ransome's definition also distinguishes it from that of an act of leisure. The word 'work' is also used to describe job description or place of employment. Due to its varying use, I use work as both a noun and a verb within this chapter. This denotes the changing nature of the work paradigm. It allows for the recognition that other aspects of lifestyle, such as leisure, are shifting into the arena of work and transforming concepts of work ethics.

Utilising the ideology of a work ethic highlights the vicissitude of the work discourse. Ransome writes that:

> ... if an important constituent part of the concept of work is a work-ethic of general beliefs about society and our role within it, there is a clear implication that by participation in the organization of work individuals are endorsing these wider beliefs.[4]

A familiar example is the Protestant work ethic. This 'ethic' linked worker morality with personal success and a desire to work for God. Developed in the seventeenth and continuing well into the twentieth century, this 'ethic' was such that:

> With the consciousness of standing in the fullness of God's grace and being visibly blessed by Him, the bourgeois business man, as long as he remained within the bounds of formal correctness, as long as his moral conduct was spotless and the use to which he put his wealth was not objectionable, could follow his pecuniary interests as he would and feel that he was fulfilling a duty in doing so.[5]

The problem is that belief structures are inequitable. Emile Durkheim suggested that 'although by constitution woman is predisposed to a life different from man ... if these differences make possible the division of labour they do not necessitate it ... for specialized activities to result they must be developed and organized'.[6] Durkheim believed that these inequalities between gender and the division of labour were only able to be performed within a situation where they were supported and developed. So although there may be differences between the genders, a division in labour becomes systematic when these differences are endorsed. Durkheim 'assumed that the gender-based domestic division of labour was a good example of the social harmony generated when social inequalities were allowed to mirror natural inequalities'.[7] This ideology of a 'division of labour' was one of the wider beliefs in existence during the period framing the Protestant work ethic. So although this 'ethic' promoted a formal working structure in the drive for economic gain, high moral conduct and religious sanctity, it was directed at the profitability of white bourgeois males. A work ethic, although enacted by the majority, is not necessarily benefiting to all. A particular example of this is that the discourse of the work ethic, containing the idea of a 'natural division of labour' does not take into account working class women and children. The Protestant work ethic, minus the religious affiliations, is a foundation for the Old Economic workplace. Women within these workplace structures adhere to it, but remain disempowered by it.

There are a few defining eras in the history of work and economic restructuring. The two major terms and concepts on which I focus are Fordism and Post-Fordism. 1914 marks the beginning of Fordism, when Henry Ford 'introduced the $5, eight hour day, working week on the first car assembly line at Michigan, in the USA'.[8] His ideologies were centred upon increasing the productivity of labour as well as the mass production of goods. His assembly line, although enabling large, widespread economic growth through maximised productivity and mass-produced goods, created unskilled and deskilled employees.

> As Fordism involved the utilisation of Taylorist principles based on the division of labour it led to the emergence of an unskilled workforce, performing highly fragmented tasks. Wherever possible Ford attempted to reduce the number of jobs requiring skill, knowledge and judgement, replacing these by simple, repetitive, unskilled tasks.[9]

This workforce model was not focused on the development of employee skills, only on how to produce goods in a highly efficient manner. Ford's eight-hour working day and unskilled workforce produced two major outcomes: a system of paid unskilled 'work' and an economy that was saturated in consumerism. Employees worked to mass-produce goods and then purchase them.[10] This created a sentiment in the Fordist society of working to play.[11] There are problems surrounding such a system of labour. The Fordist assembly line models particularly exemplify the Marxist notion of worker alienation within capitalism. Marx identifies four spheres of alienation:

> The first facet of alienation is derived from the absence of control by the producer over the product ... The second aspect of alienation stems from the ever-increasing division of labour ... The market economy and commodity exchange comprise the third facet of alienation, for they turn every productive group into competitors ... Finally, Marx asserts that the mindless repetition that typifies work under capitalism blurs the distinction between humanity and animality by destroying the creative content of production.[12]

These four spheres of alienation are enmeshed into the Fordist labour system. Workers' labour is 'fragmented' by 'simple unsophisticated tasks'. They are encouraged to increase productivity for income, which in turn promotes competition between employees and industries. The repetition of this work develops an unskilled worker who is only able to 'perform' on similar assembly lines,[13] which worked well in the period after World War II when an economy that was based on production and manufacturing was booming. Huw Beynon remarks on the job expectation in Britain during the later years of Fordism:

> I was brought up in the South of Wales, the 'jobs' available were clearly outlined and understood. There were 'jobs' in the steel works and in the coal mines. Boys who left school at fifteen or sixteen went into either of these places and became coal miners or steel workers. Those with academic qualifications became apprentices and were prepared for jobs as skilled maintenance workers in these industries. All of them understood their job to involve a powerful occupational identity and to be a 'job for life' ... There were comparatively few manual jobs for women. The girls who left school at fifteen worked as machinists in the one garment factory in the town; alternative employment was offered in local shops and, for those with some academic qualifications, in the local 'council offices'. The strong expectation was that young women would marry and not return to employment.[14]

This is reflective of the Australian model. A similar trend is found in the structure of the Australian workforce, which had a multitude of manufacturing jobs to fill during this period. Christopher Wright states that:

> Male work predominated in much of manufacturing, backed by the prevailing view that heavy, dirty or machine-based work was naturally suited to male workers. By contrast, in areas such as textiles, clothing and footwear, pharmaceuticals, food processing, and clerical work, managers tended to employ female workers, given a perception that tasks involving minimal heavy lifting and a high degree of repetition or manual dexterity were both physically and mentally more suited to women.[15]

A change in labour and employment structuring occurred in the 1970s, resulting in the demise of the manufacturing sector. This marked the beginning of Post-Fordism.

Post-Fordism did not signal the end of Fordism. The Fordist system of work is still recognisable in areas of manufacturing, hospitality, retail and throughout the service industry. As many of these positions within the era of Fordism were dominated by female workers it is questionable if Post-Fordism affected them as much as it did men.[16] It did, however, restructure the workplace and ideologies of work with the employers opting to recruit a 'higher skilled' workforce. With the arrival of Post-Fordism 'buzz' words such as downsizing, outsourcing, relocation and teamwork gained cultural currency. Wigfield explains this trend, suggesting that 'the search for labour flexibility has led to a need for a smaller but more skilled "core" workforce and a less skilled and quite vaguely defined "peripheral" workforce'.[17] Assembly lines were dispersed to geographical locations where labour was less expensive. The Post-Fordist workplace structure, involving downsizing and production relocation, left many of the 'Fordist' assembly line employees without 'work'. Although normal full-time jobs still existed for some, there was an increase in part-time and casual employment within the general workforce. In Australia, in the late 1980s, this employment trend was matched by a decline in the acceptance of trade union activity by companies. It marked the end of the 'job for life' and increased unemployment anxiety.

By the 1990s, 'globalisation' was the new buzz word, description and explanation affecting workplace structures. Stephen Frenkle asserts that:

> Globalisation was changing workplace relations in ways that were as yet not well understood. This prompted three subsequent studies of multinational subsidiaries. The cooperative dependence pattern was explored further by distinguishing between Neo-Taylorist and Lean Production manufacturing variants. There was a general tendency towards the latter pattern characterized by increasing management and technical expertise and systems integration, more complex work, greater employee involvement and weak or non-existent trade unionism.[18]

At this time, the restructured workforce consisted of multiple highly skilled managers and a 'team' of employees knowledgeable in changing technologies. Those 'underling' jobs once given to the masses were now being outsourced to logistics agencies. Under-employment, over-employment and self-employment, known collectively as non-standard employment, were now career paths that had to be considered; they defined a different 'job' formula and established a new work ethic. Under the guise of 'labour flexibility', non-standard work has both disadvantages and benefits – depending on what end of the scale an employee is located. Kim Hoque and Ian Kirkpatrick stipulate a division within the UKs contingent workforce:

> … with low-paid and poorly trained workers at one extreme and professional occupations on fixed-term or temporary contracts at the other, 'where pay is higher than average and there are high levels of human capital'.[19]

Hoque and Kirkpatrick suggest that there are similarities with all forms of non-standard work, such as lack of career advancement and marginalisation – especially for women.[20] Although there are similar ramifications for both ends of the contingent workforce, there is greater impact at the lower end of the scale. Many have experienced non-standard employment as shop assistants or service industry workers when they were at school, or in post-secondary or tertiary education.[21] It is the rudimentary stepping-stone to move into different industries and better paid places of employment.[22] The movement to, and away from, transient work is only an option if an employee's socio-economic status allows for such a transition to be made. There are some employees who remain at the lower end of the non-standard workforce for life. Hoque and Kirkpatrick write:

> Management decision-making is often influenced by stereotypes of non-standard employees as less committed, less reliable and – in the case of part-time employees – unsuitable for promotion.[23]

In such positions there is generally a relative lack of job security, as well as no holiday or sickness benefits. For high-end temporary or contract employees, this is counterbalanced by an income that is usually higher than their full-time employed peers and matched with titles such as project officer or consultant. These are not generally on offer at the lower end of the scale. This has become unacceptable for the current generation of employees, for two main reasons: the New Economy and the popular cultural workplace.

The 1990s mode of globalisation was facilitated by digitisation and convergent media, which in turn created an expansive growth in the Information Technology industry. Phrases such as 'the age of information', 'information superhighway' and 'world-wide-web' became ubiquitous. The 'pink ghettos'[24] of the computer and IT industries were being masculinised and in America, the New Economy workplace was arriving. Ross remarks, 'as rising productivity coincided with the internet boom in the last few years of the decade it became common to identify all digital or online companies as New Economy and all brick-and-mortar firms as Old Economy'.[25] The New Economic paradigm, besides its obvious links to capitalism, sparkled with early Marxist ideals. Employees regained control over productivity, skills were being enhanced and creativity flourished. The shape of the workspace also changed, evolving from the life styles of programmers and computer geeks. And as a result of unusual working hours, workspaces became places of leisure as well as 'work'. Liz Nickles asserts that:

> The philosophy seems to be: Just because you work in a pressure cooker, it doesn't have to look or feel like one. In fact, for those who practically live at the office, it makes sense to provide the comforts of home, whether that means an on-premises kitchen to whip up an omelette, a VIP spot under your desk for your dog, a twenty-four-hour media rec room, or, on lesser budgets, a chance to paint your unfinished door-desk any colour you choose.[26]

The animation company PIXAR provides an example of this, where employees play football and ride the corridors on scooters.[27] Such a change was meant to promote a comfortable and 'family' environment, which in turn would stimulate productivity by making working long hours easier. This economy is based on the creativity and talent of its workers. Historical markers of success such as the suit and large offices have been replaced with accessories that make the employees comfortable. Professionalism is embodied in the creative process and the quality of the final product or service, not in whether the employee looks stereotypically professional whilst producing it. Ross remarks that employees working in these kinds of spaces 'vowed to pursue similar working conditions, or seek ways of creating anew, even if their career paths led to corporate employment outside the orbit of the new media industries.'[28] An environment such as this sounds utopian. A 'good job' is the ambition of prospective employees.

There are a number of problems with New Economy workplaces and the first is that generation X and Y believe that they are instantly entitled to a job with a relaxed workspace, a large income and plenty of incentives. Nickles writes:

> The attitude is pervasive and has moved beyond the Internet space. For instance, in the legal area, Web sites such as Greedyassociates.com, a site for law associates, have sprung up so that entry-level lawyers can

make sure they are up to the minute with the salary and benefits status quo.[29]

Not every child is raised in a house that professes that they will be rich and successful. The origin of this sense of instant entitlement is important. Donny Deutsch suggests that it has evolved from a media illusion and that 'these are kids who grew up of a media age, and it is what they saw around them, on TV and in the news. It is what gets written about because it is sexy and exciting.'[30] Although there are not many 'pure' New Economic workspaces in Australia, generation X, Y and beyond are aware of such workplaces and the ideologies of entitlement enclosed within them. Every worker is 'entitled' to good working conditions and an interesting environment, but this form of metaphoric penthouse entitlement extends beyond the idea of a 'good job'. Workers leaving school or university expect a 'great job' and executive-level bonuses. There is no longer the 'pay your dues' ideology of the Old Economy. This transformation is due in part to the solicitation of such 'New Economic' ideals within the popular cultural workplace. These environments are depicted in popular television through situation comedies and dramas.

The popular cultural workplace is categorised by the disintegration of physical workplaces. An example comes from the popular cultural workplace presented in the popular HBO series *Sex and the City*. Workplaces are rarely frequented for sustained periods by the four female characters. It is this lack of attendance to work that illuminates the correlation between freedom of time and career success. There is no delineation between workplace and social attire. The employees are transient, successful, sociable and have large disposable incomes. The boundaries between work and social life are blurred with sexual relationships between employees, colleagues and clients. *Sex and the City* provides a significant example of the successful woman in the popular cultural workplace. Defined by their clothing, party invitations and sexual encounters, these women reset the televisual boundaries of what it meant to be thirty, single, successful and in a profession. These sculpted women were blessed with careers that the viewers rarely saw. The New Economy and the popular cultural workplace resonate and dialogue. Both exhibit a change in the definition of workspace through entwining work and leisure and increasing the visibility of casualness in terms of hours and dress. There was a certain aesthetically driven ideology that tethered aspects of an employee's everyday life – work, dress, technology and leisure – together. Recognising the link between these everyday elements is significant, not because they were not important before digital technology, but because Web 1.0 and 2.0 tied them together in a unique manner. Elements of an employee's life that had previously been compartmentalised were now a 'mashup'. Digital technology added an element of freedom in terms of leisure, work and workplace. The New Economy and popular cultural workplaces alluded to certain social values and provided a utopian formula for work that encompassed lifestyle.

Digitally present

Digital technology is a significant element of New Economic environments and the popular cultural workplace. It was a defining factor in the appearance of the New Economy, in terms of the IT industry and Internet start-ups. Digitised technology such as laptops, the Internet and mobile phones are also present in the popular cultural workplace. In *Sex and the City*, these devices are what provided the four characters with mobility in their jobs. Contemporary workplaces as ascertained earlier in this chapter are largely still Old Economic environments. Digital technology, in terms of Internet start-ups, 'funked' up the office and tweaked Old Economic aesthetics in terms of workplace attire, creative jobs, non-standard hours and ideologies of entitlement, but markers of this old system, such as professionalism, work ethics and the corporate ladder remained. The result is the non-standard workforce, which is highly dependent on, and influenced by, digital technology. Digital technology is used to conduct business day to day, and social networks are a part of this.

The use of social networking sites in workplaces is a contentious issue and demonstrates a clash between Old Economic and New Economic ideals. There are three ways that social networking websites are linked to the contemporary workforce. First, the networks themselves are representative of a second wave of Internet start-ups. Secondly, they are used in different capacities at work. Thirdly, the stability and accessibility of the digital presence that is added to outside of work can influence a user's workplace. These three factors are entwined and indicate the two-way flow of information between a user and their digital presence.

Social networking websites fall within the category of Web 2.0, which represent the second wave of Internet start-ups. Lacy writes, '… starting in 2002, came the Web 2.0 crowd … They were a bit too young to be the founders in Web 1.0 wave, but were old enough to have been dotcom rank-and-file employees and share holders.'[31] This second wave is considered to transcend the use of the Internet for just information purposes. Web 2.0 was given its label at a conference in 2005:

> The concept of 'Web 2.0' began with a conference brainstorming session between O'Reilly and MediaLive International. Dale Dougherty, web pioneer and O'Reilly VP, noted that far from having 'crashed', the web was more important than ever, with exciting new applications and sites popping up with surprising regularity. What's more, the companies that had survived the collapse seemed to have some things in common.[32]

Web 2.0 is a collection of applications that require an engagement with the web. Wilde writes that it refers to 'any application which focuses on a participatory way to use the web. In all these applications, content is collectively produced by taking existing content and adding annotations and/or context to it.'[33] Social networking sites are an example of participation with the Web. Users interact within the network in various capacities such as updating their profile, interacting with other users' profiles, contributing to group or fan pages and using applications that are linked to the network. The aesthetics of Web 2.0 start-ups resemble those that defined Web 1.0 and the New Economy. Digg is an example of a Web 2.0 application. 'Digg surfaces the best stuff as voted on by our users. You won't find editors at Digg — we're here to provide a place where people can collectively determine the value of content and we're changing the way people consume information online.'[34] Digg spawned *Diggnation*, an Internet television program hosted by Kevin Rose and Alex Albrecht. 'Diggnation is a weekly tech/web culture show based on the top digg.com social bookmarking news stories.'[35]: Kevin and Alex sitting on a couch, with their laptops, drinking beer and talking about the Digg stories from the week that have been popularized by web users. Rose, as both a co-founder of Digg and a host of *Diggnation*, is a visible example of an employee of the New Economy. For example, in 2006 Digg's Kevin Rose made an appearance at a Web 2.0 Conference at the Palace Hotel in San Francisco.[36] Lacy writes: 'he does a fifteen-minute speaking gig, with his usual two-day patchy beard, ruffled hair, and hipster garb'.[37] Rose is a poster boy for the popular cultural workplace and the New Economy. Digital technology provided a platform for his idea to come to fruition and *Diggnation* now has a legion of followers.

> The fanboys worship because he's successful but comes across as just a slightly better version of themselves. They watch Diggnation

and imagine they too could just hang out with Kevin on his couch, drinking beer and talking about girls and the Apple iPhone.[38]

IT professionals, like Rose, generated these new networks and not only rekindled the fires of New Economic workplaces, but also changed the way that Internet users participate on the Web.

One marker of the New Economic workplace is the reduction of boundaries between socialising and work. The use of social network sites in the workplace is another indicator of the changing shape of workplaces.

> Jason Greaves, director of commercial staffing at Manpower UK, says the world of work is changing. 'The explosive growth of social networking sites provides a new way for people to communicate with each other and, although the primary use of these sites seems to be for personal reasons, employers and employees alike are now using the sites for work purposes, which can save both time and money.'[39]

Although there are specific business networks that have been set up for online business networking, I will focus here on those whose primary basis is for socialising. There are two main reasons for contention regarding the use of social networks in the workplace. The first is the problematic nature of unsanctioned use of websites and the second is the impact on the level of work that is produced because of social network usage.

There is concern regarding the use of social network sites within workplaces because of the way that these platforms operate.

> A recent Forrester survey found that 78% of IT organisations are concerned about the risks of employee-driven, unsanctioned use of Web 2.0 tools and technologies. 'The primary reason is that social networking tools and services (like other Web 2.0 services and technologies), were designed to work in what Gartner calls "global-class environments," which implies open and highly scalable deployments. In order to fit within the protected "walled garden" nature of corporate environments, these services, technologies, and tools need to incorporate "enterprise class" services, such as security, access control, and auditing, before employees can use them safely within the corporate world.[40]

Social networks in the workplace are problematic due to the nature of the platform. The technology needs to be scrutinised and monitored so it does not negatively impact on other technology in the workplace. The technological structure of these networks, when situated in the context of a workplace, highlights another point of concern regarding privacy on these networks. Besides the technology, the way in which employees use these networks is controversial.

The use of social networks by employees in the workplace is of concern because of the amount of time spent, as well as the information that is being disclosed, on them. It is difficult to monitor time spent on networks such as *Facebook*, *MySpace* and *twitter* because these can be accessed via an employee's computer or phone, and as Buck asserts, 'people have always used the telephone to make personal calls, or undertaken pointless errands to gossip, the difference now is that because people are at their desks, it's harder to know when they're not working'.[41] Buck also acknowledges issues with the disclosure of company information on these networks. 'In 2003, Michael Hanscom was fired by Microsoft for posting a photo on his blog, showing badly stored computers at a warehouse.'[42] This example shows the negative impact that these networks have on the workplace itself. It also displays the two-way flow of information between the user and the network. The photograph was taken at work, uploaded to his profile, viewed by his employer and the result was the loss of his job. In some organisations, companies have banned the use of social network sites in the office altogether.[43] Although banning the use of networks in the workplace might seem like the simple solution, Lavenda argues that doing this it is at the peril of the corporation.

> Social networking is an irreversible mega-trend. As part of the 'IT consumerisation' wave, social networking is permeating organisation boundaries, with or without corporate blessing. Organisations can either ignore this trend (at their peril) or develop a strategy to leverage the trend to be more successful.[44]

As Lavenda suggests, the social network phenomenon is here to stay, so there is a definite need to incorporate usage into workplaces in some way. A survey conducted in 2008 reveals that the presence of these technologies in the workplace is now influencing people's choices of potential employers. Nick Abrahams and Paul McKeon write:

> In the Deacons' Social Networking Survey 2008, almost half of those who used social networking sites at work said that if given a choice between two jobs equal in all other respects, they would choose an employer which allowed access to these sites over one which did not.[45]

Employers are then left in a difficult position. Networks can negatively impact on the workplace due to differing standards of technological platforms and their use, but they are becoming a defining factor of workplace choice. There can, however, be a positive side to social networking in the office. As Ashley Hall reports, 'aside from retaining staff, there's another reason for employers to consider embracing social networking sites. A new study has found that people who browse the Internet for leisure at work are 9 per cent more productive than those who don't'.[46] Corporations must decide whether this reported increase in productivity is more important than the potential for negative publicity. Both Buck and Lavenda are in agreement that corporations need to find a solution. This is in terms of either reviewing organisational policies relating to Internet use[47] or creating and/or adopting new networking technologies.[48] Whatever the decision a company makes, it is clear that as these networks become increasingly embedded in a user's workplace, the potential for the digital presence to affect a user's life continues to grow.

Workers use social networks in the office for socialising, but these networks are also being used by employers to find out information about current and potential employees. Although employees are happy to use networks in the office, they are less happy about being checked up on.

> New research by recruitment firm, Manpower, has found that over half of all social network users would consider it unethical for employers to use the sites, such as Facebook, Myspace and Friends Reunited, to research potential and existing employees.[49]

The reality of networks being used by employers as a research tool, where information about employees can be gathered, signifies the importance of the information added to a digital presence outside of workplace hours. The information uploaded can affect not only a user's current position, but prospective employment as well. The digital presence, as discussed in previous chapters, is something that has a stable online existence. It is for this reason that the information added to it outside of working hours can have more of an impact on a user's working environment than its presence as a tool for socialising in the workplace.

The influence of a digital presence on the working aspect of a user's life is of importance when placed in the context of contemporary working environments. With non-standard and longer hours, employees are spending a large portion of their everyday life in the workplace. Therefore, the way in which they are perceived in the workplace will have a significant affect on their life. The level of this impact was recognised in

Chapter three, in the exposition of celebrity participation in social networks. I concluded that how celebrities interact in online social networks and the evolution of their digital presence enabled them to solidify a fan-base, advertise their achievements, and garner both positive and negative attention. The ramifications of the cycle of information that exists between a celebrity and their digital presence demonstrates the potential impact of the two-way flow of information between the average user and their digital presence. It is available to be looked at, and engaged with, by others when a user is offline. The various ways that a digital presence can affect a user's work are not dissimilar to celebrities. The influence of the digital presence evolves through the information shared and a user's relationship with their fan-base.

In Chapter four I discussed the 'social' side of social networking and revealed that a significant portion of socialising is focused on the interaction between 'friends' and 'followers'. I established that the choice of 'friends' could be viewed as a user's link to celebrities or a marker of popularity. Friendships in social networks have the positive aspect of providing the user with an online social network, but those people befriended online can influence a user's working environment offline. Although not a red pill, blue pill *Matrix*[60] moment, the decision as to whether to add a workmate, or employer, as a friend is important. Deciding to add a workmate to an online social network can be tantamount to making a private profile public, as a user is putting their digital presence on show. Sydney call centre worker Kyle Doyle is an example of this:

> A CALL centre employee has come unstuck after his boss caught him bragging about 'chucking a sickie' on his Facebook profile. Kyle Doyle's attempt at claiming a sick day after a big night out was the talk of Sydney yesterday, with an email exchange between the 21-year-old and his boss circulating in office blocks across the city. 'Kyle Doyle is not going to work, f... it – I'm still trashed. SICKIE WOO!' he posted on his profile after failing to turn up to work.[50]

Doyle's employer, AAPT, dispute that this email exchange ever took place and although it unclear whether this was a hoax or not, it does highlight the influence of allowing colleagues access to a user's digital presence. Doyle was not fired for fibbing on *Facebook*, but there have been many stories of those who have been 'busted' when their excuses did not match the actions of the digital presence. Kelvin Colvin was reprimanded when in an email to his boss he alluded to a 'family emergency' as an excuse for not going to work and then uploaded a picture to *Facebook* of himself in a Halloween costume from a party he had attended on his day of leave.[51] *Facebook* is not the only social network that can affect the lives of employees ... or potential employees. *Twitter* uses have also suffered repercussions as a result of voyeuristic employers.

> With the the [sic] thin veil of illusion privacy gently draped across said applicant's keyboard and computer screen, this bright light decided it would be a great idea to say the following: 'Cisco just offered me a job! Now I have to weigh the utility of a fatty paycheck against the daily commute to San Jose and hating the work.' To which a representative of said internet company, one Tim Levad, happened to stumble upon and respond to said 'Fatty' with appropriate consternation and a good dose of tough love: 'I'm sure they would love to know that you will hate the work. We here at Cisco are versed in the web.'[52]

There have been numerous accounts of employees being reprimanded or fired for expressing their opinions of work in their profiles. Kimberley Swan of Essex was fired from her job when she remarked that her job was boring on her *Facebook* profile. 'Details were passed to her employers after she allowed colleagues access to her page, Miss Swann said, adding that she was not given the chance to explain.'[53] Thirteen Virgin staff were fired for 'criticising the airline's flight safety standards and describing its passengers as "chavs" on a social networking website'.[54] It is clear that, as well as the private/public status of a profile, the decision to add colleagues as 'friends' is not one that should be taken lightly. The other side of the 'friendship' coin is to not add your work colleagues at all. However, given the level of social network use in the workplace, for both business and socialising, this could also raise issues relating to mistrust or feelings of social isolation. Business journalist Myles Wearring believes, 'it's a good idea to create two profiles – a professional one for your work contacts and clients which doesn't include too much private information, and a personal profile where you can muck around with your friends and family'.[55] Wearing's suggestion is only a partial solution, as there would be workmates who are friends as well that had access to both profiles. The solution then is for a user to self-monitor the digital presence.

The first step in controlling who views a user profile is to ensure that it is private and not public. Monitoring a digital presence can be achieved either by adapting privacy settings or by controlling and removing content from the network. Although quite time-consuming, adapting the privacy settings in a social network can help to control how much information is shared, and monitor who has access to it. Changing privacy settings is more complicated than setting up two profiles because, in a network such as *Facebook*, the user has to add people to groups and then only allow certain groups to view particular information. Monitoring information allows the user to stop certain 'friends' or 'groups' from viewing material such as status updates, news feeds and photographs. Although controlling privacy settings in a social network like *Facebook* can reduce the impact of a digital presence in the user's workplace, this is not so for all networks. If a user blocks access to updates on *twitter* then they are blocking access to their entire account. Also, if a user blocks access to *twitter* after they have already had a public profile, 'updates posted previously may still be publicly visible in some places'.[56] The alternative is to control the information that is actually available on your profile. *MySpace* allows the user the option of pre-approving comments before they are posted to the profile[57] and within their safety guidelines they state:

> Don't post anything that would embarrass you later. It's easy to think that only our friends are looking at our MySpace page, but the truth is that everyone can see it. Think twice before posting a photo or information you wouldn't want your parents, potential employers, colleagues or boss to see![58]

Not disclosing any compromising information is probably the best way to reduce the impact of a digital presence on a user at work. Although a digital presence is a stable presence that is always available online, the user still controls what is they upload. So another option is to delete the information after you have posted it. If a user needs to rant or update their status with something controversial, then leave a time limit to how long it is up there – a day, an hour, five minutes – then remove it. There are also issues regarding monitoring a digital presence in terms of the removal of context. The argument could then be made that deleting some posts and not others can have the added affect of seemingly harmless material being left on a profile that is taken out of context. However, returning to the concept of context (in relation to social networks) that was discussed on Chapter three, the act of uploading short updates combined with the structure of the networks means that whatever information is available on the networks can always be misread. Monitoring, however, can reduce the opportunities for information to be taken out of context. Monitoring a digital presence to such an extent might seem excessive, but it is clear that social networking is being used in, and impacting on, workplaces and for this reason extreme rigidity may be the only option for reducing the severity of its influence over how employees are perceived. Boundaries between work and socialising are being obscured, but Old Economic protocols of professionalism still exist. The digital presence that is shaped in social networks can challenge acceptable office behaviour, and for this reason if colleagues are a part of this network, then it needs to be monitored.

The chat function that is available within a social network is not easily monitored. It is the underbelly of social networks. There is an ease of (mis)use that is found in the instant and quick form of communication that is provided by chat functions. These conversations cannot easily be monitored or recorded and are easily deleted. It is for this reason the content disclosed within them is usually unrelated to work. The chat function is a clear marker of the New Economy's focus on leisure, but it questions professionalism and ideologies of work. The chat function is what I would call an everyday undercurrent. Given that this service is provided through a social network, rather than a business chat client, there is always going to be a 'social' element to these conversations. This social element, coupled with the ease with which content can be deleted, marks it as a controversial element to have in a workplace environment. The significance of the chat function as an undercurrent is discussed in depth in the next chapter.

Through an exploration of the protestant work ethic, Fordism, Post-Fordism, Old Economy, New Economy and the popular cultural workplace, I have demonstrated a variety of differing working conditions and values that directly influence current workplaces and use of digital technologies therein. A look at contemporary workplaces has revealed how Web 1.0 and the rise of the New Economy brought a fresh and creative aesthetic to contemporary workplaces. Although Old Economic ideals of professionalism and corporate ladders are clearly still present, the New Economy offers a glimmer of hope regarding work delivering more than a job for life. This was exemplified in texts such as *Sex and the City* with the arrival of the popular cultural workplace. The popular cultural workplace was characterised by New Economic working conditions such as non-standard working hours and mobility through digital technology, and showed how socialising crossed the boundaries between work and home. This workplace encouraged unrealistic expectations but was an indicator of how 'socialising' is an important part of work and a desirable factor in contemporary workplaces. The development of Web 2.0 and the rise of social networks not only rekindled the creative New Economic conditions brought about by Web 1.0, but it also brought a new form of socialising into workplaces. This in turn has led to issues regarding the extent of socialising in the office and its impact on productivity. It has also revealed the two-way flow of information from the user to their digital presence and how this presence can affect a significant part of the user's life, namely work. For this reason social network usage needs to be monitored. Employers must decide whether these networks are used in the workplace. Employees need to be exacting in their choice of 'friends', privacy settings or the information that is disclosed. Social networks are used in many workplaces for business and socialising. These spaces are a clear example of how the digital presence can permeate the offline world in a significant manner. Therefore, the onus is on the user to choose how they use these networks, as they must consider the different ways that the digital presence influences their life.

Notes

1. Ross, A. (2003) *No-Collar: The Humane Workplace and Its hidden costs.* New York: Perseus, p. 1.
2. *Ibid.*
3. Ransome, P. (1996) *The Work Paradigm.* Aldershot, UK: Avebury Press, pp. 16–17.
4. *Ibid.,* p. 75.
5. Weber, M. (2002) T. Parsons (trans), *The Protestant Ethic and the Spirit of Capitalism.* London: Routledge, p. 120.
6. Durkheim, E. (1997) *The Division of Labour.* New York: Free Press, pp. 264–5.
7. Grint, K. (1998) *The Sociology of Work.* Malden, MA: Polity Press, p. 98.
8. Wigfield, A. (2001) *Post-Fordism, Gender and Work.* Aldershot, UK: Ashgate Press, p. 7.
9. *Ibid.,* p. 8.
10. *Ibid.,* p. 9.
11. This is not ignoring the fact that many workers actually worked to survive.
12. Grint, *op. cit.,* pp. 87–8.
13. Michael Moore confirms this in the documentary *Roger and Me.* He showed that the workers that Ford had laid off in Flint could not 'manage' the pressure of the fast food industry. M. Moore (dir) (1989) *Roger and Me.* USA: Dog Eat Dog Films & Warner Brothers.
14. Beynon, H. (1997) 'The changing practices of work', R. Brown (ed.), *The Changing Shape of Work.* New York: Macmillan, pp. 20–1.
15. Wright, C. (1995) *The Management of Labour: A History of Australian Employers.* Melbourne: Oxford University Press, pp. 50–1.

16. Wigfield, *op. cit.*, p. 50.
17. *Ibid.*, p. 52.
18. Frenkle, S. (2002) 'Workplace relations: past, present and future'. *Australian Journal of Management*, 27(SI): 155.
19. Hoque, K. & Kirkpatrick, I. (2003) 'Non-standard employment in the management and professional workforce: training, consultation and gender implications'. *Work, Employment and Society*, 17(4): 669.
20. *Ibid.*, p. 670.
21. Erica Smith writes: 'Typically, children commence with jobs in the "informal" economy such as paper rounds and babysitting, progressing on to formal jobs in the service sector jobs, typically in fast-food outlets and shops. Formal part-time work whilst at school is now a common experience for school students in Australia. The latest data (from 1997) suggests that among teenage students (including teenage university students), around 30 per cent of males and 40 per cent of girls worked part-time. Smith, E. (2000) 'One foot in the workplace'. *Australian Trading Review*, 34: 15.
22. *Ibid.*
23. Hoque & Kirkpatrick, *op. cit.*, p. 670.
24. 'Pink Ghettos' refer to employment areas that are dominated by women.
25. Ross, *op. cit.*, p. 9.
26. Nickles, L. (2001) *The Change Agents*. New York: St Martins Press, p. 29.
27. Docter, P., Silverman, D. & Unkrich, L. (2001) *Monsters Inc- special features*. USA: Pixar.
28. Ross, *op. cit.*, p. 15.
29. Nickles, *op. cit.*, p. 15.
30. *Ibid.*, p. 15.
31. Lacy, S. (2008) *The Stories of Facebook, YouTube & myspace: The people behind, the hype and the deals behind the giants of WEB 2.0*. Richmond, UK: Crimson Publishing, p. 53.
32. O'Reilly, T. (2005) 'What is Web 2.0?', available at: *http://www.oreillynet.com/lpt/a/6228* (accessed 6 July 2009).
33. Wilde, E. (2008) 'Deconstructing blogs', *Online Information Review*, 32(3): 401.
34. Digg (2009) available at: *http://digg.com/* (accessed 8 July 2009).
35. Diggnation (2009) available at: *http://revision3.com/diggnation/* (accessed 8 July 2009).
36. Lacy, *op. cit.*, p. 113.
37. *Ibid.*
38. *Ibid.*, p. 275.
39. Anon. (2007) 'Workers show naivety over online presence', available at: *http://www.internalcommshub.com/open/news/manpower.shtml* (accessed 13 July 2009).
40. Lavenda, D. (2008) 'Does "blogging" have a place in the workplace?'. *The British Journal of Administrative Management*, July: 27.
41. Buck, J. (2007) 'Managing the rising use of social networks at work'. *Strategic Communication Management*, 11(6): 8.
42. *Ibid.*
43. *Ibid.*
44. Lavenda, *op. cit.*, p. 28.

45. Abrahams, N. & McKeon, P. (2008) 'Media release: employers taking chances when blocking Facebook too, says Deacons', available at: *http://www. deacons.com.au/legal-services/technology-media-telecommunications/ media-releases/media-release.cfm?objid=6383* (accessed 13 July 2009).

46. Hall, A. (2009) 'Facebook "good for productivity", in moderation', transcript available at: *http://www.abc.net.au/news/stories/2009/04/02/2533719.htm? section=features* (accessed 13 July 2009).

47. Buck, *op. cit.*, p. 8.

48. Lavenda, *op. cit.*, pp. 27–9.

49. Snell, A. (2007) 'Do you Google Your Candidates?', available at: *http://www. taleo.com/talent-management-blog.php/2007/11/06/do_you_google_your_ candidates* (accessed 4 July 2009).

50. *The Daily Telegraph* (2008) 'Kyle Doyle busted after sickie brag on Facebook', available at: *http://www.theaustralian.news.com.au/story/0, 25197,24539147-5006784,00.html* (accessed 4 July 2009).

51. Thomas, O. (2007) 'Bank intern busted by Facebook', available at: *http://gawker.com/tech/your-privacy-is-an-illusion/bank-intern-busted-by- facebook-321802.php* (accessed 4 July 2009).

52. Truemorist (2009) 'Forget Layoffs, Cisco Fatty, Tweets Will Keep You Unemployed', available at: *http://www.nowpublic.com/culture/forget- layoffs-cisco-fatty-tweets-will-keep-you-unemployed* (accessed 4 July 2009).

53. BBC News (2009) 'Facebook remark teenager is fired', available at: *http://news.bbc.co.uk/2/hi/uk_news/england/essex/7914415.stm* (accessed 4 July 2009).

54. Conway, L. (2008) 'Virgin Atlantic sacks 13 staff for calling its flyers "chavs"', available at: *http://www.independent.co.uk/news/uk/home-news/virgin- atlantic-sacks-13-staff-for-calling-its-flyers-chavs-982192.html* (accessed 4 July 2009).

55. Wearring, M. (2007) 'Is Facebook good for the workplace?', *News.com.au.*, *http://www.news.com.au/business/story/0,23636,22437742-5012427,00.html* (accessed 4 July 2009).

56. Twitter (2009) 'Profile Settings', available at: *https://twitter.com/account/ profile_settings* (accessed 15 July 2009).

57. MySpace (2009) 'All User Safety Settings', available at: *http://www.myspace.com/ safetyaustralia* (accessed 15 July 2009)

58. *Ibid.*

59. Parton, D. (1980) '9 to 5' Singing for the Common Man. Nashville, TN: RAC.

60. Wachowski, L. (1999) *The Matrix*. USA: Groucho II Film Partnership.

6

You've been poked: bullying, harassment and everyday undercurrents

A few years ago a friend who was new to *Facebook* asked me: 'what is a poke? Is it bad or good?' In my naivety I had assumed it simply meant to virtually prod someone, a form of an annoying but friendly 'hello, come talk to me'. Until then the fact that it could be used to irritate or as a form of flirting had never crossed my mind. Poking to me had seemed liked harmless fun, but its potential to incite irritation, or be used as a sexual invitation, stopped my poking in its tracks, and a new side to social networking was revealed to me. Within the friends and frivolity of games and conversations lay the potential to be harassed. Bullying and harassment have become common within social networks, ranging from minor disagreements between friends, to stalking and serious cyber-bullying and harassment. This chapter discusses the darker side of social networking. I begin this exploration by looking at cyber-harassment and bullying within social networks. I then discuss identity theft relating to corporations and personal harassment. Cyber-bullying and harassment are crimes that are not only becoming more prevalent on social networks, but are something that can have tragic consequences, and it is for this reason that these are focal points of this discussion. The topic of cyber-bullying is an important part of this book because it not only reveals the power of social networks, but also highlights how embedded these networks are in our lives. My discussion then moves from the stirring, monumental and tragic events that have been widely broadcasted through the media, to the negative experiences that affect a user's everyday life. The second half of the chapter is dedicated to exposing the everyday undercurrents that are present in social networks. I use three personal examples to show how features such as status updates, photographs and the chat function are undercurrents. It is the use of these seemingly positive features that highlights the potential for negative experiences to occur. This chapter shows that it is the everyday engagement with these networks that permanently locates the user on the precipice of infelicity.

Identity theft is defined by Roberts as:

> ... the online misappropriation of identity tokens (e.g. email addresses, webpages and the combination of username and password used to access systems), typically for financial gain. Other identity-related information that can be readily harvested online include names, contact details and, in the United States, Social Security Numbers.[1]

When an identity is stolen on the Internet, it is often with the purpose of procuring financial information, which can result in financial corporations being viewed as the 'victim' rather than the individual involved. Roberts asserts, 'organisations (defrauded creditors) are often regarded as the primary victims of identity theft exposure'.[2] This form of identity theft, in terms of defrauding a predominantly unknown user for financial gain, is victimisation. Cyber-harassment, however, becomes far more intrusive when identities are stolen with the purpose of undermining the user.

In a previous chapter I discussed the idea of identity theft in terms of impersonating an individual. The presence of celebrities on networks such as *twitter* and *Facebook* demonstrated how this impersonation can result in undermining and controlling public perceptions of the 'real' person. Identity theft can be just as crippling for In non-celebrities. Kaitlin Keane reports on one example of a Norwell teenager who had her identity stolen by two other school students.

> The Facebook profile bore her picture and her name. Like 80 million other profiles posted on the social networking site, it listed her supposed activities, interests and a group she had started.
>
> But none of the offensive information posted on the popular site in February had actually come from the freshman girl whose face graced the page. The profile only remained online for one day, but the words caused enough harassment online and in school hallways to drive the girl from the school and turn her life upside down. Now, two of her former classmates face criminal charges that they committed identity fraud in order to harass the girl, and they could get up to 2½ years in a house of correction.[3]

Identity theft in this case resulted in cyber-harassment, cyber-bullying and bullying at school. The end result was that this student had to change schools. This type of identity theft, albeit brief, is emotionally damaging and is becoming more common. Ki Mae Heussner reported on a recent case in Illinois:

> What would you do if someone impersonated you on Facebook, amassed hundreds of friends and then used the site to tarnish your reputation? An Illinois mother says that's what happened to her teenage son, and the two are striking back with a lawsuit. In a 20-page document filed with the Circuit Court of Cook County, Ill., Sept. 23, Laura Cook and her son, a minor identified only as 'John Doe,' allege that four pranksters created a fake profile page impersonating the plaintiff that included racist and explicitly sexual comments ... 'We've seen a number of [civil] cases being brought recently when cyber harassment occurs,' said Parry Aftab, the executive director of WiredSafety.org, an Internet safety resource. Aftab said she said she was aware of approximately 100 similar cases across the country in the past year.[4]

This form of harassment involves teenagers most commonly, because their skills on the Internet and digital communication are relatively advanced. Yet this technological literacy is not matched with the same level of social literacy. Carolyn D. Baker, in reference to nursery learning, asserts that:

> Classroom reading practices create their own discourses and orders of knowledge: in the examples presented here these appear to be discourses and knowledges about the interiors of stories and about world-knowledge, but not about texts. If literacy is understood as methods for talking about, characterising, and analysing *texts* as such (cf. Olson & Astington in press/1990), this raises the questions of whether students are encountering literate discourses in these classroom reading events.[5]

The text in question here is the Internet in general and social networks more specifically. I have articulated in previous chapters that although there may be resources such as netiquette guides for interacting online, it is still a space of moral ambiguity, which I believe is due to a misunderstanding of the impact of online environments. I suggest this is due to the presumed anonymity of the Internet where, within this social context, it would appear that identity is not sacred. The actions of identity thieves and bullies on the Internet are a tangible part of 'real' life. Although information contained within social networks is generally snippets of a user's like, it is still a part of the digital presence. In terms of social literacy, the ramifications – emotional, physical and legal – need to be learned because the results of cyber-harassment and bullying are often dire.

Cyber-bullying can occur easily within social networks. It can be defined as 'the use of email, text messaging, web sites, discussion forums and other technological means of communication to intentionally hurt, defame or intimidate another'.[6] Although anybody has the potential to be bullied, it has been the relationship between teenagers, social networks and bullying that has been most well publicised. Powers writes:

> The prevalence of Internet use among young people has opened up a new stomping ground for the playground bully, a ground where there are no teachers and few adults to help draw the line between acceptable and unacceptable behaviour. The ease with which most teenagers use technology like cell phones and computers makes it far too easy for one child with a grudge to turn life into a living hell for another student.[7]

The difference between cyber-bullying and (old) playground bullying is that the victims cannot remove themselves from it in the same manner. They cannot leave it behind in the playground and be free from it within the safety of their own homes. As Powers suggests:

> Unlike schoolyard bullying, there is no 'safety zone' when you're the victim of a cyberbully. It's almost impossible for the victim of a cyberbully to control the situation by walking away from it. The effects of being virtually bullied are every bit as real as those of being made the laughing stock in a real world situation.[8]

Although I agree with Powers' sentiments, her last sentence highlights the belief that somehow there is a tangible boundary between on- and offline environments. Cyber-bullying is a real-world situation. What happens online does not stay online, yet there seems to be some underlying assumption that information posted online is sent out into the ether, written on a virtual Etch-a-sketch, and that it is not as important, significant or real as that which is said in person. Cyber-bullying is invasive and confronting. That a person has taken the time to put into writing how they feel about another, simply to digitally defame them, is of course a concern. Ria Hanewald writes:

> Qing Li, however, argues that cyber bullying is in a new territory of the virtual world, where it appears 'safer,' limited to words and pictures, thus causing 'only' emotional and psychological but not bodily harm. Of course, the impact of cyber violence on the victim might be far greater than the impact of face-to-face bullying. Media report and anecdotal evidence show that cyber bullied victims suffer from poor academic performance and a range of stress related symptoms like anxiety, sleeping problems and depression.[9]

The emotional damage caused by cyber-bullying highlights the *reality* of a user's relationship with the Internet. Social networks fit into the cyber-bullying debate because they provide a space with multiple levels for contact where this behaviour can take place. Chat, walls, blogs, comment boxes and email are all different avenues for contact – some require friend requests but many do not. One of the reasons why cyber-bullying is so prevalent is linked to my previous assertion that there is some anonymity with posting information online. As Kate McCaffrey puts it, 'another characteristic of this form of bullying is the anonymity it provides. It allows children who probably would not engage in this behaviour to hide behind the faceless nature of the Internet and torment others.'[10] However, it is not just teenagers who are undermining user identities and bullying online.

Megan Meier was a 13-year-old, who after being dumped by a *MySpace* 'friend', was then harassed within the 'bulletin' area of the site. She subsequently hanged herself.

> Thirteen year old Megan Meier committed suicide after being intentionally befriended and then dumped by someone she believed to be a new online friend named Josh Evans. In reality, Josh Evans – who said he was new to the neighborhood – turned out to be a MySpace account created by the mother of a schoolmate of Megan's. Megan and the child had once been friends.[11]

Lori Drew, the mother in question, said 'she had created the *MySpace* profile because she wanted to gain Megan's confidence to know what Megan was saying about her own child online'.[12] Later charges against Drew were dropped because

... the primary reason that so many people were upset by the conviction of Lori Drew is because one of the convictions was based on her violation of the MySpace terms of service (TOS), and there was a 'the sky is falling' response, with people worrying that it meant that violating a site's terms of service could mean criminal prosecution for all.[13]

Users want to keep their privacy, hold back personal information and remain protected, yet the very policies put in place to do so are violated so easily; fake surnames, ages and locations, for example, do little to protect actual lives.

Interaction with social networks amplifies the gulf between on- and offline life that many users presume exists. The impact of the digital presence on a user's everyday life is extensive, and so it should be recognised that given the amount of time spent within these networks, negative experiences are going to weigh on a user just as much as the positive. Social networks are so pervasive that it is difficult to believe that these cases are purely naive occurrences where the perpetrator did not know how these networks operate. Those controlling what goes in social networks are in a position of power. Anonymous bullies can manipulate identities and use words to victimise users, but although bullies might know how and why they are using these networks – for instant, directed and faceless intimidation – they cannot control the outcome. The facelessness of the Internet means that bullies cannot gauge a response or have a visual indicator that they may have gone too far. Social networks mean so much to some users and so little to others, so behaving inappropriately within these networks is going to vary between users. Baudrillard suggests:

> Video, interactive screens, multimedia, the Internet, virtual reality – we are threatened on all sides by interactivity. What was separated in the past is now everywhere merged; distance is abolished in all things: between the sexes, between opposite poles, between stage and auditorium, between the protagonists of action, between subject and object, between the real and its double. And this confusion of terms, this collision of poles means that nowhere – in art, morality or politics – is there now any possibility of moral judgement. With the abolition of distance – of the 'pathos of distance' everything becomes undecidable. And this is true even in the physical realm: when the receiver and the source of a transmission are too close together, a feedback effect ensues which

scrambles the transmission waves; when an event and the broadcasting of that event in real time are too close, this renders the event undecidable and virtual, stripping it of its historic dimension and removing it from memory.[14]

This is true of the relationship between the user's digital presence and social networks. People and various facets of their life have been drawn together in a manner that mirrors socialising and friendship, yet this interaction operates in an arena that is treated as if it is outside of moral ramifications, which I believe is related to the presence of a screen. Perhaps in terms of transmission, as Baudrillard suggests, a scrambling is occurring in the relationship between a user and their digital presence. The Internet and social networks are constantly evolving and becoming more pervasive, yet user social literacy has not caught up. Although there may be netiquette and guides for networks such as MMORPGs there is no single edict for how a user should act online and 'social networks' seem to be the Ibiza of the Internet. The growth of cyber-crime is linked to the growth of the Internet as a cultural, social and emotional part of everyday life. Therefore, how users approach the Internet and social networks, in terms of social literacy, needs to change accordingly.

Social networks and their links to suicide and murder is a subject that has garnered much media attention over the past five years. Teenage suicide is often linked to social networks, because they are sites of cyber-bullying and also places used to plea for help, vent emotions or leave a final note. A suicide pact between Jodie Gater and Stephanie Gestier was highly publicised in Australia in August 2007. The pact was substantiated with posts left on Gater's *MySpace* page. 'It reads: "It's over for me, I can't take it! I hear it over and over again. It feels like it always rains." Another of Jodie's MySpace websites reads: "Let Steph n me b free".'[15] The insidious nature of social networks and the varying degrees of interaction with them makes it difficult to gauge when a friend is being over-dramatic about their feelings by posting something like 'Uggh I want to die' or are actually writing a cry for help or goodbye message. Kevin McGee, ex-partner of *Little Britain*'s Matt Lucas, left the note 'Kevin McGee thinks death is much better than life'[16] on *Facebook* before committing suicide. After his untimely death his friends, unaware of what had occurred, were still posting messages on his *Facebook* page. 'One who commented on his brooding message wrote: "That's a bit dark, Kev!"'[17] How to act appropriately becomes unclear in areas of bulk communication. There is an awareness of the types of information that should not be uploaded – racist, sexist, pornographic – to social networks. Boyd writes:

> Social convergence occurs when disparate social contexts are collapsed into one ... Social convergence requires people to handle disparate audiences simultaneously without a social script. While social convergence allows information to be spread more efficiently, this is not always what people desire.[18]

Due to this lack of a social script, users can often find themselves teetering on the edge of inappropriateness when sharing information. It is how material is shared and the amount of 'everyday' information that is shared that can make social networks socially unstable and potentially personally damaging.

Social networks and their links to murder have also been highlighted by news media. In September 2009, 'Welsh-citizen Brian Lewis is accused of strangling his partner Hayley Jones to death in the home they shared with their four children. Prosecutors argue that the crime was precipitated by the amount of time Hayley spent on Facebook and her burgeoning social horizons.'[19] This is not the first time that *Facebook* has been implicated in the murder of a user. In 2008, 'a man murdered his estranged wife after becoming "enraged" when she changed her marital status on Facebook to "single"'.[20] Although clearly the depths of the issues in these two relationships are unknown, the role that *Facebook* had to play was not. These sites are soapboxes and it is through their everyday use as such that issues arise. An example of this is the simple change of a relationship status from 'single' to 'in a relationship', to 'married', then removed or the reverse. These simple changes can set digital tongues wagging and congratulatory/condolence messages flying. It is through the concealment of user information, or the absence or tweaking of information, that a glimpse of the surreptitious and sordid side of these networks is seen. Boyd asserts that 'people relish personal information because it is the currency of social hierarchy and connectivity. Cognitive addiction to social information is great for Facebook because News Feeds makes Facebook sticky. But is it good for people?'[21] The amount of information shared and how a user interacts in an 'everyday' manner is where the true extent of how the digital presence that is manifested in these networks really impacts on a user's life.

Social networks have become so embedded in our lives that we do not realise the extent to which they influence us. They are an insidious force that allows an intimate form of communication which would otherwise not exist. In some ways this is positive because it can allow a user to feel connected to a world that they are physically disconnected from. However, the nature of the information that is communicated via the different layers of interaction allows for doors to be opened into users' lives that may have otherwise been left closed. It is only by observing the depth and way that information is shared within a social network that we can truly realise the consequences of using them. Simmel discusses the conflict that occurs in the web of group affiliations. Given that a user's social network can contain multiple social circles, it seems that conflict is inevitable:

> As the individual leaves his established position within *one* primary group, he comes to stand at a point at which many groups 'intersect.' The individual as a moral personality comes to be circumscribed in an entirely new way. But he also faces new problems. The security and lack of ambiguity in his former position give way to uncertainty in the conditions of his life. This is the sense of an old English proverb which says: he who speaks to languages is a knave. It is true that external and internal conflicts arise through the multiplicity if group-affiliations, which threaten the individual with psychological tensions or even a schizophrenic break.[22]

Social networks mark the intersection of a user's (social) group-affiliations. These friends are often privy to the same information and same updates, yet outwith the networks these 'friends' do not play the same role in a user's life. This is the same for the user. They are given so much information from their friends, but do they want to know that much? On the surface these networks add value to a user's life. They provide friendship, companionship and a form of social life, but in fact they give so much more. They give the user knowledge and opportunity to interact with people in ways that, within the framework of social networking, are normal, but outside of that context could be considered inappropriate.

Everyday undercurrents

I have been a social network user for many years and prior to this I used many forms of Internet chat programs and email. The difference between social networks and other forms of Internet communication is the insidious nature in which they operate. Social networks appear to be open spaces where information is laid bare in what is often presumed to be an honest environment. Notes are posted to walls, email chains are written like speech bubbles, and photographs are tagged and commented on. Once a user is friends with someone this gives them the opportunity to involve themselves in that person's life in a way that would otherwise be impossible. Although these spaces are created for fun and networking, the choice of the information uploaded and the way that it is shared creates a world of influence that is both delightful and treacherous. I have had three personal experiences that demonstrate how a digital presence can leave a user questioning the appropriateness of communicating within a social network.

The first demonstrates how easily common communication practices that are the currency of social networks can stray from friendly banter to something more serious. This example began when I innocently updated my *Facebook* status with the question: 'What book should I read next? I need some new reading material.' Various friends chimed in with suggestions of books that they had read or their favourite authors. One of my very close friends listed several books she thought that I might like. She then jokingly made reference to 'graphic novels', which she knows that I do not read. My friend had a dig at me about not considering these texts – given that I am a writer. I ignored it for a few hours and then that evening (after a couple of glasses of wine and what I believed to be in the spirit of joviality) my husband and I both responded to her post regarding 'graphic novels' with grand irreverence. Her response to our posts was curt and sarcastic. I assumed that she was just irritated about being 'put in her place', but I later learned that it went far deeper than this. My friend's posts were then replaced by her husband's and what began as a thread about new reading material quickly changed into a three-way war of words about the stupidity of the phrase 'graphic novel'. In the end my husband, myself and my friend's husband agreed to disagree and we amicably ended the thread.

My friend and I, who have known each other for ten years, would always comment on each other's *Facebook* pages, send emails and text message each other every few days. This all stopped. I quickly noticed her absence from my digital world and after a week I sent her an SMS to see if she was annoyed with me. What ensued was a series of messages about what had occurred on *Facebook*. I had assumed that she had thrown down the gauntlet by her remark that questioned my writerly attributes, and so I was of the opinion that we were conducting one of our usual 'anything goes' sarcastic repartees. These were the normal types of conversations that we engaged in when we were all face-to-face. My friend, however, felt that my husband and I had bullied and attacked her. She thought we were premeditated in our attempts to publicly humiliate her. This was not so, but when reading and reflecting on the whole thread it was easy to see why she thought this was the case. Text takes time to write. A user can perfect the ultimate quip and edit their work so that they post the punchiest and most scathing one-liners. Words are the currency in these networks and users mould and play with them as you would any equipment that is required for a leisure activity. My friend was hurt because she saw *Facebook* as a public arena and she believed that I would not treat another user the way I treated her. My immediate reaction was defensive. She had started with a small jibe and, yes, I most probably would have had the same argument with others. The fact that I was writing this book made me reflect on this situation for a moment and look at the context of the conversation. She had posted her remark from her house in the afternoon. She was five months pregnant and sober. I let her post eat away at me for hours as it stared back at me from my profile wall. I let it aggravate me to the point of anger. This (alcohol-fuelled) anger led me to sit down and construct a response that not only vilified her comment (which attacked me as a writer) but which also publicly challenged her intelligence. It was all there for my friends to read. Every user who had posted a comment prior to this argument would have been notified each time one of us responded within the thread. What had started out as a textual repartee ended as a carefully worded debate, where we tore strips off each other's use of language and play on words. With time and resources a user can forge the perfect sentence but without facial expressions, gesticulation, vocal tone and physical presence these words can be ill-received. There are not enough winking emoticons in the world that can capture the sarcastic or dramatic tone with which a post has been written, and in my case it was only through speaking to my friend and seeing each other that the strained bonds of friendship could be fully restored.

The second experience that I had on *Facebook* demonstrates how the joys of sharing every aspect of your life with friends can change in an instant. As I have already discussed, sharing pictures within social networks forms a large part of profiles and building a digital presence. Photographs provide a visual snapshot of a user's life. Photograph albums are used to track and share the various occasions and journeys in users' lives such as festivals, weddings, holidays and pregnancy. These 'joyous' events are captured and presented within the network for friends to enjoy and comment on. Pregnancy is a common 'journey' that is often chronicled on *Facebook*. Updates about morning sickness, rants about weight, and pictures of ultrasounds and expanding stomachs become a publicised pregnancy diary. I myself spent many hours on *Facebook* in the final days of my pregnancy. A week before my due date I began a countdown and I also used it as a soapbox to complain about my discomfort. During the bulk of my pregnancy, however, I did not upload many photographs of myself or unborn child. The few that I did were kept in private albums for my interstate and overseas girlfriends. From past experience of losing a child part of me knew that pregnancy is an uncontrollable thing and in a way so is the information that is released into a social network. I held back on uploading images because if anything bad happened during my pregnancy I did not want to have to explain it to people with whom in the majority I was just an acquaintance. If something had happened I did not want to have to log into my profile and see a happy picture of myself with a pregnant belly. I controlled what I uploaded because I could not bare tragedy to be a part of my *Facebook* experience. I felt I could not share this part of my life on *Facebook*, but some people do.

Early in 2009 I logged into my *Facebook* account and checked the news feed. I noticed that several of my friends were posting messages of sympathy to one of my other friend's profiles. I knew that this friend was 38 weeks pregnant and in an instant my stomach hit the floor. I used the webmail function to email my other friends. Both emailed back to tell me that my friend had lost her baby. I was devastated for her. I knew her pain as I had felt it before. I looked at her *Facebook* page and her whole pregnancy lay before me. I not only wanted to take her pain away but I also wanted to tear down her profile. Obviously this response was coloured by my own experiences and I was projecting how I would feel if I was her. All I could think was that this woman was going to log in and see the whole journey from joy to tragedy. In my mind it was too much. How much of our lives do we really need to expose? I also wondered how you move forward within a network after this has happened. My reaction would have been to want to remove my profile but as discussed in previous chapters these networks are a part of everyday lives. Friendship, bonds and comfort are drawn from these spaces. A week or so passed and I logged into *Facebook* as part of my normal daily ritual; I checked the news feed and I began to cry. Then I bolted from my room. The first images I had seen when I logged in were pictures of my friend's stillborn baby. I cried out of shock as memories from my past shot to the surface. I cried for my friend's tragedy and these final images of her journey. I had not been ready to receive this information. I did not choose to receive this information. It was thrust upon me before I had a chance to breathe.

Within an hour my friend had changed the initial photograph of her and her baby from her profile picture and put a link to them in an album. After my own shock and confusion I contemplated this brave move of hers to upload these photographs. She had every right to upload them. This was her journey to share – the good and the bad. This was her choice and by me entering into a 'friendship' with her in the network I also chose to see all aspects of her life. However, we do not necessarily know the ins and outs of other people's lives. We do not know if the information that we upload challenges or upsets them. My friend made a brave choice to upload those photographs. They shocked me to the core but they showed the utter rawness of reality. She did not just upload the perfect pictures of her life to the network, she spoke the truth of it to everyone and it was at this point I realised that I did not.

The information overload that occurs on *Facebook* is largely due to the structure of the News Feed. The News Feed is, as boyd suggests, what makes this network 'sticky'. In relation to this abundance of information sharing she writes:

> Biological programming makes us believe that individuals who are sharing personal details are indicating trust. In an unmediated society, social currency is a means to building a relationship. People reciprocally tell each other about their family, thoughts and desires. Friendships are built on mutual knowledge of each other's lives and the lives of those they know. Social and emotional support is one of the outcomes of such friendships.[23]

This begs the question of what friendship actually means within social networks. Although I agree with boyd that there is a level of trust that is given to allow 'friends' to view a user profile, I believe that this is a false sense of trust. At the time of accepting a friend, trust is given, but then with the expansiveness of the network many of these friendships then fly beneath the 'trust' radar. I do not believe that each user actually sits there and thinks about their hundred plus friends before they upload a picture of themselves, family or friends. The idea that a temporary trust exists within social networks reinforces my previous suggestion that social networks are a space of moral ambiguity or what boyd, with regard to *Facebook*, refers to as a 'grey zone'. She writes:

> There is an immense gray area between secrets and information intended to be published as publicly as possible. The assumption

was that if you were visiting someone's page, you could access information in context. When snippets and actions were broadcast to the News Feed, they were taken out of context and made far more visible than seemed reasonable. In other words, with News Feeds, Facebook obliterated the gray zone.[24]

I believe that the grey zone still exists on *Facebook* and, in particular, on *twitter*. Even when posts are read within a profile, the user is limited with the amount of information they can post (in terms of the amount of context they can provide to all 'friends') and they also have the ability to monitor information (delete, rework, repost). The multiple avenues for public and private communication that *MySpace*, *Facebook* and *twitter* offer mean that context may be provided to some users but not others. A user does not necessarily know who is accessing their information, or for what purpose. Nor do they know what information they will receive from a friendship. Social convergence can continually lead the user into sticky situations, which can leave them questioning the idea of privacy within such networks.

The first two experiences I have described portray the 'public' problems associated with communication within private profiles. They explain the negative and difficult experiences that can occur within the everyday use of social networks. I have described these experiences in order to show how common and easy it is for positive encounters to turn into negative life-altering events in an instant. Bullying, stalking and suicide are very striking examples of the extent to which social networks can negatively impact not only a user's life but also the lives of their families. The insidious nature of these networks, however, reduces the visibility of the common elements of negative activity that occur within them. These are the everyday undercurrents such as small fights, jibes, photographs that you did not want to see, posts that you read before you realised that you did not want to read them, videos that you watched in good faith but ended up leaving a sour taste in your mouth, and conversations posted to your wall or tweeted to your profile that should have never entered this domain. These undercurrents can leave a user questioning whether they want to be part of such a machine.

The chat functions found in social networks are pertinent examples of the negative impact of everyday undercurrents. Internet Relay Chat programs, instant messaging clients, email and now social networks have been around for many years and within the context of online communication and chat a certain 'naturalisation' of these form of interactions has occurred. Social networks, however, bring another aspect to these forms of communication because they not only work as modes of communication but they also are constantly evolving a user's digital presence, and portray the chosen parts of a user's life through uploads to the profile. Networks are also heavily based on 'friendships' and without these there would be no interaction and no people to network with, but as soon as a user enters into a relationship with each person they are opening themselves to scrutiny. They are choosing to expose themselves and be exposed to each other. Obviously there are many value-adding reasons for engaging in this behaviour but it is in the very operation of social networks that allow for unnatural relationships to be forged. As previously discussed, within private profiles there are very public experiences, and it is through these that both joy and unhappiness can be presented. There is also a very private side to these networks, where notions of social appropriateness are really challenged.

Facebook, *MySpace* and *twitter* provide users with the ability to send each other private emails/direct message. *Facebook* and *MySpace* users also have the ability to chat to one another privately. The chat function is an excellent example of how a simple tool for instant communication can place a user on the precipice of inappropriate behaviour. Within the context of social networking and other forms of online communication, instant messaging functions are the norm. They allow a user to instantly connect with their friends or colleagues. They help users to get answers quickly. These functions allow a more natural form of communication because, in a sense, they are like talking. Interactions are more or less instant and conversations can flow. Unlike the wall, there is less chance for misunderstanding because although words are still carefully crafted, any ill-received remarks can be fixed instantly. So chat allows a user to craft their words but also provides them with the opportunity to quickly reword and apologise if words are taken out of context. Context is an important element of this discussion because it is only one part of social networks, and as social networks are like leisure centres, chat also needs to be looked at as a leisure activity. This leads me to my third experience.

I have spent many hours using chat clients. These forms of communication have been a part of my socialising and as such I have always seen them as significant and positive. Outside of social networks the reasons for logging into chat clients like MSN Messenger has always been very clear – I was logging in to chat. When you log into a social network, with their multilayered forms of communication and other leisure activities, you are not always going there to chat. However, if you are on a network like *Facebook* and your status is always set to 'online' you are always available to chat. People log into chat clients to chat.

People log into social networks for a myriad of reasons. The chat function is an unobtrusive box at the bottom of the screen, barely noticeable among the adverts, quizzes and applications. You do not actively have to go and login to the chat – one click on this box and you are online. If you want to go offline, then you must actually go into the program and select to do so. In this way it is easy to always be available. Not that opting to be offline is difficult, but one click and you are again online ... suddenly you are in a conversation.

I would like to reflect here on the positive sides of social networks. Users go into them to socialise and for the most part have 'fun'. They are leisure centres where people interact, usually in a public manner. The number of friends available is vast and how a user selects their friends is of great importance, a point provided by my next example. In Chapter five I discussed the complications that can arise when social networks become part of the workplace. The chapter largely focused on the changing shape of the workforce and the ill-defined boundaries that now exist between leisure and workspaces. Social networks further blur these boundaries and the choice of work colleagues as friends, as noted, can lead to issues regarding a user's digital presence. It was argued that the actions of this digital presence can lead to issues regarding professionalism, losing face, friends and even jobs. These various repercussions are all highly visible within a workplace environment. By this I mean the consequences are as noticeable as the actions that led to the employee being scrutinised. In turn, there is an inconspicuous and negative side to social networks in the private chat function. The ramifications of ill-judged use here are less visible than those posted on a wall for example.

Chatting online has never really been an issue for me and I have always seen it as a form of entertainment. I chat to people who I find interesting, organise offline catch-ups and ignore conversations with those who I find boring. I never get into chats with acquaintances, only those people I know. I have my own rules for chatting, which I have developed over many years of challenging conversations and for this reason I have never found it unusual to be talking to multiple people – both male and female – at the same time. Within my household it is ordinary behaviour for my husband and I to be chatting to people online throughout the day. This is something that until recently we never questioned.

My husband has a very select group of friends on *Facebook*, and is only friends with people he actually knows, one of whom was a work colleague. Both my husband and I spend time in the evening talking to each other face-to-face and talking to our friends online. We never hid the people we were talking to and I knew that he would often be talking to his work colleague for a few hours in the evening. We would always chat about what they were talking about – usually work. One evening he received a text message from his colleague informing him that her husband had made her 'unfriend'[25] him. Both of us started joking about it. To us talking this way, online, was normal behaviour … and I then began thinking that perhaps it is not. I explained to my husband that he did not know the circumstances under which she was talking to him. She could have been hiding it from her husband or minimising screen windows when he walked in. Chatting in this manner should be viewed like any other form of communication and they were doing this for two hours every day, after spending the day together at work. I commented about this to my husband and said: 'you spend all day at work and to him [her husband] chatting online is probably equal to spending two hours on the phone, something that you would not do. It probably seems a bit dodgy.' My husband agreed with this analogy. It was in that conversation that I realised how inappropriate these conversations actually were.

The boundaries between work and home have now ceased to exist. The insidious nature of chat allows for conversations to occur and a closeness to be forged in a manner that is easy. boyd writes: 'my hunch is that the stream of social information gives people a fake sense of intimacy with others that they do not really know that well. If this is true, it could be emotionally devastating.'[26] Yes, boyd, it is … I do not necessarily believe that it is fake intimacy, but it is a particular intimacy that is generated by the network. One of the key features of online chat is that you do not have to go into another room to talk; you can do so while chatting to your spouse, so in this way chatting for hours online seems less inappropriate. Chatting online removes the boundaries of appropriateness because of its immediacy. You do not have to make arrangements, have a reason for going out, get dressed, go out, and meet these people to hang out, have a drink and a good chat. All can be done from the comfort of your home.

There is a certain ease that exists when communicating within a social network as no one can actually see what you are doing in terms of the pages that you are looking at. There is a layer of anonymity that is attached to a digital presence, which in turn affects all aspects of a user's life. Social networks, however, go beyond communicating. They allow users to innocently lurk, stalk and generally be voyeuristic. As boyd writes:

> Unlike bloggers, most connections on Facebook are at least weak ties, but power differences still exist. Unreciprocated romantic crushes highlight the dynamic as the crusher follows the crushed

intensely without the reverse being true. Through the regular updates, the crusher develops a feeling that she knows her crush, but her crush is barely aware of her presence.

Facebook gives the 'gift' of infinite social information, but this can feel too much like the One Ring – precious upfront, but destructive long term.[27]

Boyd has pinpointed the 'grey zone', as she calls it, of these networks. No user can tell how each of their friends is reading their updates or if they are even reading them at all. It is only when we recognise the everyday engagement and negative undercurrents present in networks that we can see how insidious they actually are. For all the life that they give, they equally can take it away and a user must ask how much information is too much?

Did I really need to know that?

When reading the *Facebook* news feed I seem to be constantly asking myself versions of the same question: 'did I really need to know that?' Most of the time the answer is a resounding no. No, I did not want to know how fabulous my friend's new car is. No, I do not want to know about the saga of a friend's child's potty training and no I do not really care if someone I have not seen in ten years is drinking beer at the pub while I am at work. I do not really need or want to know. The status update is an undercurrent that is constantly moving my 'good' networking experience into a 'negative' one. On every social network the network's version of the status update is intrinsically competitive. This is because, as I discussed in earlier chapters, you would not have a digital presence or be updating, tweeting or blogging if you did not want someone to read and/or comment on it. It is a competition to be happier, sadder, meaner or have a bigger following. Users lap up this information and compare it with their own lives. They use the network and other computer functions to perfect their digital presence. Baudrillard writes:

> It is this phantasm of the ideal performance of the text or image, the possibility of correcting endlessly, which produce in the 'creative artist' this vertige of interactivity with his own object ... In fact, it is the (virtual) machine which is speaking you, the machine which is thinking you.[28]

Although this constant competition, comparison and one-upmanship regarding the banal elements of life highlights the narcissistic and negative tendencies of the network, it is only when taboo subjects enter the network that we see how other users are actually affected.

Earlier in this chapter I wrote about my sensibilities being challenged when a friend uploaded pictures of her stillborn baby. I was shocked due to my own experiences and because I saw these pictures without actually wanting to. This incident highlighted what friendship means on these networks. When you enter into a friendship you must accept the good with the bad and know that you will receive information that you do not necessarily want, and from people you would not necessarily have that level of intimacy with outside of a social network. In November 2009 controversy was caused when Penelope Trunk, in just 140 characters, nonchalantly tweeted about her miscarriage while in a business meeting. She stated, 'I'm in a board meeting. Having a miscarriage. Thank goodness, because there's a fucked-up three-week hoop-jump to have an abortion in Wisconsin.'[29] Trunk hit back at critics saying that she had tweeted about other things in her life and that people deal with emotions towards miscarriages differently.[30] Her original tweet regarding miscarriage was quite harsh and given her familiarity with social networks (she runs a networking career management website entitled The Brazen Careerist[31]), one would think that she may not have tweeted about such an important topic in such a flippant manner. This holds particular resonance given that, in her response to critics, she pushed the point that the topic of miscarriage should not be kept taboo as it disempowers women.[32] Trunk's response to critics discussed why she had said what she said. It provided a context and history to her situation. It was also 6228 characters long. The Trunk incident is a pertinent example of an everyday undercurrent not only negatively affecting her 'friends' who were offended by her comment, but also herself. The tweet was also posted while she was at work. Posting in this way is a part of her work, which highlights the impact of social networking on Trunk's workplace. Trunk's tweet illustrates how these undercurrents are an inherent problem in the social network system. First, communicating on a topic in this manner highlights the difficulty with expressing tone in a short update. Secondly, it reveals the ramifications for the user when a post is deemed inappropriate in terms of requiring a clean up and an in-depth explanation. Finally, it brings to light the idea that these networks generate too much information and that when a user is 'friends' with someone they relinquish their control in terms of the information that they receive. When all is said and done the users that followed Trunk chose to do so. They chose to follow and read her tweets and in doing so opened themselves up to a wealth of information that they did not necessarily want.

The computer screen is a boundary and the Internet an emotional minefield. As digital technology moves, we harness and engage with it, but we still carry sensibilities, emotions and social mores. We all have our own world views and beliefs, and yet we invite people into our everyday lives who we do not know and let them shape our days with information that we do not necessarily want. The structure of the Internet and social networks provides us with the ability to communicate constantly. It hints at a certain level of freedom – friendship, leisure and work – yet a user is still bound to the realities of their everyday life. Their views and beliefs do not change simply because they are communicating in a social network. So as user 'you slip on your own life like a data suit'.[33] Yet the presence of the screen creates a 'grey zone' in terms of social rules, a morally ambiguous space that expands as the ability to communicate information grows and we live more life through the screen. Baudrillard suggests:

> It is only with the strict separation of stage and auditorium that the spectator is a participant in his/her own right. Everything today conspires to abolish separation: the spectator being brought into a user-friendly, interactive immersion. The apogee of the spectator or his/her end? When all are actors, there is no action any longer, no scene. The end of aesthetic illusion.[34]

The different parts of our lives are being drawn together through the screen (a phrase which Baudrillard rejects), in what is a user-unfriendly manner. I articulated in previous chapters that there is a two-way flow of information between a user and their digital presence and that the digital presence is always linked to the realities of the user's life. In the discussion regarding work, I put forward the idea of a user monitoring their digital presence. This allows a user to control the information that they disclose. To take monitoring one step further a user can use the different network functions to ignore, block or hide information disclosed by their friends. These functions still only allow a user to limit a certain amount of information that they receive, as they are usually deployed after the offensive information is seen. The information that is shared within these networks filters into the rest of a user's life, so given the abundance and often negative amount of information that is fed through social networks, the eventual desire to remove oneself from them is an obvious transition.

I have established in earlier chapters that it is the engagement with others, by communicating and socialising about the information shared within these networks, that provides the user with a sense of a 'social circle' and positive feelings of well-being and friendship. The way that information is shared, however, can have the opposite affect on users. This chapter looked at cyber-bullying and harassment as examples of highly mediated negative experiences that have been linked to social networking sites. There are, however, other under-emphasised forces at work within social networks that mean, by simply having a digital presence, a user is constantly on the precipice of a negative experience. By using my own personal experiences I showed that everyday undercurrents such as status updates, photographs and chat, which are the elements which develop a user's digital presence and are key elements of positive networking, are also tools for social and emotional destruction. These undercurrents are so important because they are another element of the network's lifeblood and it is their constant presence and everyday use that masks their negativity. One tasteless update or inappropriate photograph might temporarily upset your morning coffee, but if this is happening every day then the social value provided by the networks diminishes. These everyday undercurrents challenge the presumption that increased communication, made available through social networks, is necessarily positive, which was highlighted in the discussion of the Penelope Trunk tweeting incident. The abundance of information being shared and communicated leaves a user questioning the level of connectivity needed between disassociated 'friends' and acquaintances, and whether they need to be a part of an information machine. The insidious ways in which these networks challenge our everyday lives and relationships that have been articulated in this chapter highlight a need for further examination. Discussion relating to the impact of heightened levels of communication and connectivity do not fit into the scope of this book, and instead I focus my attention next on how to escape the networks altogether.

Notes

1. Roberts, L. (2008) 'Cyber-Victimisation in Australia: Extent, Impact on Individuals and Responses Briefing Paper No 6', available at: *www.utas.edu.au/tiles* p. 1.
2. *Ibid.*, p. 5.

3. Keane, K. (2008) 'Nasty Web page brings identity fraud charges in Norwell', available at: *http://www.patriotledger.com/news/cops_and_courts/x875594985/ Nasty-Web-page-brings-identity-fraud-charges-in-Norwell* (accessed 20 August 2009).
4. Heussner, K. (2009) 'Teens Sued for Fake Facebook Profile', available at: *http://www.abcnews.go.com/m/screen?id=8702282&pid=79* (accessed 30 October 2009).
5. Baker, C.D. (1991) 'Literacy practices and social relations'. In C.D. Baker & A. Luke (eds) *Towards a Critical Sociology of Reading Pedagogy*. London: Routledge, p. 176.
6. Powers, D. (2006) 'Taking aim at cyberbullying', *Education Horizons*, 9(1): 30.
7. *Ibid*.
8. *Ibid*.
9. Hanewald, R. (2008) 'Cyber safety', *Professional Educator*, 7(1): 36.
10. McCaffrey, K. (2007) 'The dark side of the 'Net'', *Information and Communication Technology*, June: p. 14.
11. The Internet Patrol (2009) 'Thirteen year old Megan Meier commits suicide after cyber bullying and online emotional attack by classmate's parents posing as child', available at: *http://www.theinternetpatrol.com/thirteen-year-old-megan-meier-commits-suicide-after-cyber-bullying-and-emotional-attack-by-classmates-parents-posing-as-child/* (accessed 7 October 2009).
12. The Internet Patrol (2009) 'Mother whose online harassment of teen lead to teen's suicide may be charged with fraud', available at: *http://www. theinternetpatrol.com/mother-whose-online-harassment-of-teen-lead-to-teens-suicide-may-be-charged-with-fraud/* (accessed 7 October 2009).
13. The Internet Patrol (2009) 'Lori Drew MySpace suicide conviction overturned', available at: *http://www.theinternetpatrol.com/lori-drew-myspace-suicide-conviction-overturned/* (accessed 7 October 2009).
14. Baudrillard, J. (2002) C. Turner (ed.) *Screened Out*. London: Verso, p. 176.
15. The Sydney Morning Herald (2007) 'Death pact teen's grim poems', available at: *http://www.smh.com.au/news/national/grieving-mother-asks-why/2007/ 04/23/1177180529637.html* (accessed 7 October 2009).
16. Brown, A. M. (2009) 'Kevin McGee, ex-partner of Little Britain star Matt Lucas, commits suicide, leaves note on Facebook', *The Telegraph*, *http://blogs.telegraph.co.uk/news/andrewmcfbrown/100012615/kevin-mcgee-ex-partner-of-little-britain-star-matt-lucas-commits-suicide-leaves-note-on-facebook/*
17. Staff Writers (2009) 'Little Britain's Matt Lucas' ex Kevin McGee commits suicide', available at: *Entertainment, http://www.news.com.au/entertainment/ story/0,28383,26172634-5013560,00.html* (accessed 6 October 2009).
18. Boyd, D. (2008) 'Facebook's privacy trainwreck: exposure, invasion, and social convergence'. *Convergence*, 14(13): 18.
19. Warren, C. (2009) 'Did Facebook jealousy lead to murder?' available at: *http://mashable.com/2009/09/02/facebook-murder-case/* (accessed 2 September 2009).
20. BBC News (2009) 'Wife murdered for Facebook status', available at: *http://news.bbc.co.uk/2/hi/uk_news/england/staffordshire/7845946.stm* (accessed 23 January 2009).

21. Boyd, *op. cit.*, p. 17.
22. Simmel, G. (1955) *Conflict and The Web of Group Affiliations.* San Francisco: Free Press Association, p. 141.
23. Boyd, *op. cit.*, p. 17.
24. *Ibid.*, p. 18.
25. In 2009 the term 'unfriend' was named by the *New Oxford American Dictionary* as word of the year. News.com.au (2009) 'Facebook's 'unfriend' is word of the year', available at: *http://www.news.com.au/technology/story/0,25642,26362154-5014239,00.html* (accessed 17 November 2009).
26. *Ibid.*
27. *Ibid.*, p. 18.
28. Baudrillard, *op. cit.*, pp. 178–9.
29. Trunk, P. (2009) 'Why I tweeted about my miscarriage', available at: *http://www.guardian.co.uk/lifeandstyle/2009/nov/06/penelope-trunk-tweet-miscarriage* (accessed 14 November 2009).
30. *Ibid.*
31. 'The Brazen Careerist', available at *http://www.brazencareerist.com/* (accessed 16 November 2009).
32. Trunk, *op. cit.*
33. Baudrillard, *op. cit.*, p. 177.
34. *Ibid.*

7

Are we dead yet?

Death within social networks, as previously articulated, is not new. At the end of the last chapter I had reached a point of disdain regarding social networks. Feelings of contempt can leave the user contemplating the removal of their digital presence from social networks altogether. This chapter focuses on the user's choice to become digitally dead. Moving on from suicide, this chapter commences by first looking at how social networks are used to immortalise those users who have died offline. From here I discuss the idea of becoming digitally absent. Then we come to our final resting place, becoming digitally dead. There is an industry based around removing your identity from the Internet and this chapter discusses how this relates to becoming digitally dead within a social network. I look at how a user removes themselves from *Facebook*, *twitter* and *MySpace*. Removing a digital presence is not necessarily as simple as deleting an account, so the social and psychological implications for a user are also discussed. In a world of social convergence I question whether it is indeed possible to delete a digital presence permanently.

A user's digital presence does not necessarily die when they die offline. Although the user can no longer engage in the 'action' side of this presence, information about the identity, history and previous actions of the user are still available to be interacted with. This digital presence remains in a state of suspension. The history of the user's digital presence can still be engaged with and it is probably for this reason that the profiles of users who have died often become shrines. Users' lives become immortalised on the screen. The difficulty in removing deceased accounts is a contentious issue. Lauren Williams reports:

> The morbid conundrum is a growing problem for legal professionals, who urge social networking users to keep a log of internet passwords to help executors finalise their loved one's estates. While it is not known how many of the 200 million Facebook accounts open

worldwide are 'inactive', a spokeswoman said administrators do not automatically remove personal profiles when a user dies ... While some users say the memorial sites have been a consolation, others are angry they have no power to remove the sites.[1]

Memorial sites are offered by the *Facebook* network. This entails the deceased user's account being converted to an account that hides certain information.

When a user passes away, we memorialize their account to protect their privacy. Memorializing an account removes certain sensitive information (e.g., status updates and contact information) and sets privacy so that only confirmed friends can see the profile or locate it in search. The Wall remains so that friends and family can leave posts in remembrance. Memorializing an account also prevents all login access to it.[2]

Memorial sites acknowledge a user's digital and physical death. They are equivalent to a social network funeral. However, the fact that both the user accounts and memorial sites are so difficult to remove can raise emotional issues for family and friends who do not want an everlasting wake.[3] Both *Facebook* and *MySpace* will remove deceased accounts if a death certificate is provided. *MySpace* also suggests creating a group page as a memorial account, which can be linked to the user's profile.[4] The immortalisation, through memorial pages, is a deceased user's digital death. Memorial pages are where digital friends can mourn and a level of intimacy is given to 'friends' who 'knew' the digital presence. Travis Kravulla writes of his former classmate and *Facebook* friend 'Harry' whose *Facebook* account was memorialised after he committed suicide:

In the era of online social networking, one often hears about how MySpace, Facebook, and similar websites desensitize young people to their everyday interactions. Online, the fights are more frequent and venomous, the flirtations more direct and lascivious. But until Harry, I had not yet been called upon to imagine what footprint Facebook would leave on the solemn act of remembering the dead.

Here lay our friend Harry: inside an electronic network that brings disparate mourners together, even while making them feel emotionally distant and, when they powered down the laptop, utterly alone.[5]

Memorial sites offer a space to mourn the loss of a real person and immortalise a snapshot of their life. In death, the true nature of disconnectedness and unknowingness between the user and their 'friends' is revealed. But given the nature of social networks, memorialising the digital presence seems the natural conclusion to its death in this space. A user has lived and died part of their life through the screen and so closure within this context is needed. If there is no recognition of death, then a user is simply digitally absent.

The choice (or need) to become temporarily or permanently disengaged from a social network can occur for a myriad of reasons that can be loosely categorised as addiction, affliction and boredom. Addiction to the Internet 'is defined simply by the duration and frequency of online sessions – sessions that might involve internet shopping, emailing, chat rooms, or any number of different online activities. Such addiction is in fact quite rare.'[6] I am placing addiction to social networks under the banner of Internet addiction because extensive research is yet to be published in the area. Demetroviks *et al.* argue that '*internet addiction* should be reserved for the description of excessive Internet use with clinical significance and must be separated from problematic use in general'.[7] I place problematic use, within the context of social networks, into the category of affliction. Social network addiction can then be defined as the frequent and prolonged use of the networks that results in clinical signs of addictive behaviour such as compulsion, an 'unconquerable desire to engage'[8] with the network, withdrawals and neglecting other areas of life.[9] Addiction to social networks requires clinical attention and the source of addiction must be challenged. Ergo, the user must sever their connection with the social network, which would probably require the permanent deletion of profiles from social networks. This would be a digital death rather than just a temporary deactivation or digital absence. I will examine the subject of a digital death later in this chapter.

I categorise affliction as the user's problematic relationship with the social network. Indicators of affliction may reflect addiction, such as prolonged and frequent use of websites, although an affliction involves other factors that demonstrate that the social network is negatively impacting on the user's life. Feelings of dissatisfaction and uneasiness with the network, boredom, isolation from offline friends and activities, and being 'time poor' can all amount to feelings of affliction, which in turn can lead to a digital absence. Boredom is the final and probably most common reason for removing oneself from the social network. Boredom with the networks differs from affliction because it is more about being generally unenthused with the network experience, rather than feeling specifically negative about the network itself. Chaney and Blalock argue that 'boredom may be magnified when people experience additional feelings of loneliness and depression. To escape feeling lonely or *bored*, people may access the *Internet*.'[10] But if a social network has nothing to offer a *new* user – no sense of community, communication or friendship – the time spent within the network can be boring. Conversely, the relationship with a social network for a seasoned user is like any relationship, and if the experience becomes predictable and mundane it can also become boring. Affliction and boredom can leave a user toying with the idea of absenting themselves.

In the context of social networks there are two ways that a user can be digitally absent. The first is to leave a profile online and not engage with it, and the second is to temporarily deactivate it. A digital absence differs from a digital death in that it presupposes a return to the network at some point, so deactivation of a profile is not the same as removing the profile altogether. The two forms of digital absence are dependent on intention. A user might not be engaged with their digital presence because they are on holiday, sick or have a lack of access to the Internet. The deactivation of an account is a definite indicator that the user wishes to be digitally absent at that particular time. Throughout this book I have discussed the positive and negative aspects of a digital presence and being digitally absent has similar life-affecting elements. When a user separates themselves from social networks, they are able to reflect on their relationship with them.

A user's digital absence affects both the user and their 'social network'. A digital absence allows the user to reflect on the role that social networks played in their life. It allows a user to recognise the magnitude of their digital presence and how this presence shapes and is shaped by participation in online social networks. A hiatus from a network can also enable the user to identify whether they have an addiction or affliction. It can help the user to focus on what they want from social networks and what they are actually receiving from them. A digital absence allows for distance and reflection. Reflecting on the current and desired relationship that a user has with these networks forces the user to recognise how they use the network, how much time they spend on it, and what they are actually gaining from participating in it.

The extent to which a digital absence affects the user's social network is only truly recognised when the user becomes present again. For example, after a brief sojourn offline I updated my profiles. I was then inundated with messages of concern from my 'friends' who were 'worried' about my absence. A digital worry perhaps? No one attempted to contact me outside of the social networks during this time, so it seemed that it was my return that marked my absence. I was questioned as to why I had not updated my status recently. Had I been ill and was I ok? This recognition of my absence startled me. It made me realise that I had not simply been using the network, but I was contributing to it. An obvious revelation perhaps, but one for which the extent is not known until a user stops participating. The networks may have affected me but I also affected them. Present or absent I was giving life to this social organism. A digital absence allows for reflection on the relationship between the user's digital presence and the network. It is only when we have been in a relationship, stepped back and reflected upon it that we can actually see our function within it. My absence from the network allowed me to see how much time I wasted during the day – updating my status and playing *Scrabble* (and it was wasting time, because these activities were not adding value to my life, but simply a form of trivial socialising and communal procrastination). I was not using the network to obtain a positive 'social' experience. My absence highlighted my contribution to the network, which was to stimulate and participate in social communication. This did not, however, make me feel loved or appreciated for my wit, humour and scintillating conversation, because I knew exactly what my updates were – a combination of rants, affirmations and song lyrics. It merely revealed that it is the banal elements of the everyday that makes these sites function. Nobody will comment if I do not post the itinerary of an overseas trip, change my profile picture for a year or upload video of my children. Users will, however, notice if I do not update my status for a week. Procrastinating about your digital presence is a narcissistic pastime and when the revelation eventually comes that these networks are reducing a user's quality of life, the moment has arrived to make an absence permanent.

Digital death or 'webicide' is when a user permanently removes their digital presence from the Internet. Each social network has a different form of webicide. *Facebook* allows the user an absence by way of 'deactivation' of a profile. This means that:

> ... your profile and all information associated with it are immediately made inaccessible to other Facebook users. What this means is that you effectively disappear from the Facebook service. However, if you want to reactivate at some point, we do save your profile information (friends, photos, interests, etc.), and your account will look just the way it did when you deactivated if you

decide to reactivate it. Many users deactivate their accounts for temporary reasons and expect their information to be there when they return to the service.[11]

In order to permanently delete an account on *Facebook* a user must log in and make a request. Once a request has been made there is no option for recovery. Removing an account from *twitter* is a far simpler process. All a user needs to do is select 'delete account' in their profile settings. In terms of recovery this means:

> Deleting your account removes your profile from Twitter. After deletion, associated account information (such as user name, email address, etc.) is unavailable for use. If you wish to use your user name or email address with a future account, be sure to change them in your settings page before you delete your account.[12]

Committing webicide within a social network seems permanent. The way that the websites speak of the subject is with trepidation; for example, *twitter* writes 'Good ... bye?' It is as if they are questioning the user's desire for a digital death, 'Do you really want to do this? You know it's permanent right?' It is referred to colloquially as webicide because it is intentionally killing a digital presence. *MySpace* has a similar process to *twitter* in that a user needs only to go into their account settings in order to 'cancel' their profile, but again the wording of the removal advice is laden with textual stalls:

> Hey, we hate to see you go. Keep in mind that cancellation is permanent. Once you delete your profile, you can't get any part of it back! So if you're not sure, you might want to set your profile to private (so it's only visible to you). That way, you can re-activate your profile quickly if you change your mind and still have all your friends, playlists and photos available. Plus, you'll still be able to enjoy cool features like MySpace Music and Video.[13]

Killing your profile within a social network is really only partial webicide in terms of a digital presence. In order to completely remove a presence entirely, all digital traces would have to be removed from the Internet.

Given the rate at which users upload information to the Internet, it is unsurprising that there is a lot of information 'out there' on how to remove it. Bots, spyware and general Internet usage horde user information, which turns up in searches on such websites as Google and Yahoo. If a user is intent on removing their digital presence altogether then they must take the time to trawl the Internet looking for and deleting their information. Google and Yahoo can help a user with this. Google has a 'web removal tool'.

> Use the URL removal tool to request that information be removed from Google Web Search and Image Search results. You can use this tool to request the following types of removals:
>
> - Remove outdated or missing webpages.
> - Remove information or images.
> - Report inappropriate content appearing in SafeSearch filtered results.
>
> We'll investigate and provide an update on the status of your request as soon as possible. Removals that are processed through this tool are excluded from Google search results for six months.[14]

It is important to note that these removals are only for six months. Does that mean a user has to undertake these requests every six months to prevent their digital presence being immortal? Yahoo has a similar tool that allows 'for your authenticated sites, you can now delete any URLs from the index. Simply locate the URL in Site Explorer and click on the "Delete URL" button. The URL and all its subpaths will be deleted shortly thereafter.'[15] Deleting information that you have uploaded is just one element of identity removal. There is also a lot of information available that individual users do not have the authority to delete.

Smashgods.com provide some helpful advice about removing information from the Internet in 'Become Web Dead: Erase Your Online Identity in 10 Steps'. These steps begin with deleting what you can first, contacting employers and webmasters and asking them to remove information, then suggests using various free web removal options and websites (ReputationDefender, hidemyass and ChillingEffects), as well as paid identity removal services (RemoveYourName.com) and finally propose the only way to truly kill your digital presence is to stay off the Internet.[16] Staying away from the Internet is not easy to do because it is embedded in everyday practice. Email, instant messaging and workplace online networks are all a part of a user's daily life. Employers use it to find out information on potential employees and as ReputationDefender states:

Who you are online is as important as who you are offline. Naturally, professionals, parents, teachers, college applicants, graduate school applicants, job seekers, employers, and daters have raised serious and legitimate concerns about how to deal with this reality and with the ever-increasing amount of information about each of us on the Internet.[17]

The extent to which the Internet and social networks infiltrate our lives cannot be ignored simply because we do not like them or do not wish to use them. A user can, to some extent, control what they upload, what stays online, and how they interact with the Internet and its sub-networks.

Given the extensive use of the Internet in everyday life, a more realistic approach would be to view and use the web with a developed social literacy. Users need to interact with the Internet to communicate at a level that does not challenge or destroy other modes of communication, friendship and relationships, and they should only put into it what they would not be nervous about sharing with a stranger. Throughout this chapter I have looked at the downside of the social networks, in terms of value taking rather than adding. The concoction of negative experiences within social networks such as death, affliction, addiction and boredom can all contribute to a user wishing to remove themselves temporarily or permanently from social networks. Given that a digital presence, in the context of the Internet, is formed through a user's identity and actions, the task of 'killing' it takes more than just permanently deleting a social network account. There are a number of actions that can be taken to remove information from the Internet but this can take time and money. While staying away from the Internet may be the most appropriate action to take, it is not necessarily one that can be adhered to, as it is a part of everyday life. Social network sites, however, do not have to be used. We have choice. There is also a freedom in being disconnected and not having to constantly monitor or watch your back. In the context of social networks, a digital death may be the most value-adding life experience of all.

Notes

1. Williams, L. (2009) 'Cyber graveyards a growing problem for legal professionals', available at: *http://www.news.com.au/technology/story/ 0,28348,25650983-5014239,00.html.* (accessed 8 June 2009).

2. Facebook (2009) 'What does memorializing an account mean?', *http://www. facebook.com/help/search.php?hq=death&ref=hq*
3. Williams, *op. cit.*
4. MySpace, 'How can you delete or access a deceased user's profile?', available at: *http://faq.myspace.com/app/answers/detail/a_id/369/kw/death/ r_id/100061* (accessed 8 August 2009).
5. Kravulla, T. (2007) 'Death on Facebook: a different kind of funeral', *National Review Online*, *http://article.nationalreview.com/?q=ZjJhNzE3 Nzg1ZTU0ODhlODhmMjM2NmEwNGE4YTYyYjY=* (accessed 8 August 2009).
6. Wolfendale, J. (2007) 'My avatar, my self: virtual harm and attachment'. *Ethics and Information Technology*, 9: 117.
7. Demetrovics, Z., Szeredi, B. & Rózsa, S. (2008) 'The three-factor model of Internet addiction: the development of the Problematic Internet Use Questionnaire'. *Behavior Research Methods*, p. 572.
8. *Ibid.*
9. *Ibid.*
10. Chaney, M. P. & Blalock, A. (2006) 'Boredom proneness, social connectedness, and sexual addiction among men who have sex with male internet users'. *Journal of Addictions & Offender Counseling*, 26(2): 118.
11. Facebook Help (2009) 'I want to permanently delete my account. How do I delete my account?', available at: *http://www.facebook.com/help/search. php?hq=i%20want%20to%20permanently%20delete%20my%20account* (accessed 8 August 2009).
12. Twitter Help (2009) 'How do I delete my account?', available at: *http://help. twitter.com/forums/10711/entries/15358* (accessed 8 August 2009).
13. MySpace help (2009) 'How do you delete your MySpace profile?', available at: *http://faq.myspace.com/app/answers/detail/a_id/285/kw/how%20do%20 you%20delete%20and%20account/r_id/100061* (accessed 8 August 2009).
14. Google (2009) 'Google Webmaster Tools', available at: *https://www.google. com/accounts/ServiceLogin?service=sitemaps&passive=true&nui=1&conti nue=https%3A%2F%2Fwww.google.com%2Fwebmasters%2Ftools%2Fre movals&followup=https%3A%2F%2Fwww.google.com%2Fwebmasters %2Ftools%2Fremovals&ltmpl=urlremoval&hl=en* (accessed 10 November 2009).
15. Yahoo Search Blog (2007) 'Yahoo! Site Explorer: authenticate your site via a META tag and more goodies', available at: *http://www.ysearchblog.com/ 2007/01/30/yahoo-site-explorer-authenticate-your-site-via-a-meta-tag-and-more-goodies/January 30, 2007*, (accessed 8 August 2009).
16. Smashgods.com (2008) 'Become Web Dead: Erase Your Online Identity in 10 Steps', available at: *http://smashgods.com/2008/08/20/become-web-dead-erase-your-online-identity-in-10-steps/August 20th, 2008* (accessed 8 October 2009).
17. Reputation Defender (2009) 'About Us', available at: *http://www. reputationdefender.com/company* (accessed 10 October 2009).

8

Conclusion

I know that absence might
make the heart grow fonder
or is it 'out of sight'
out of mind' I wonder[1] – The Darkness

I actually consider it a cultural task not unworthy of a philosopher
to present to the broadest possible public a certain intellectual
opinion on and absorption in precisely the most superficial and
everyday phenomena.[2] – Georg Simmel

Absence is not necessarily a good or bad thing in a relationship. It is
entirely dependent on the type of relationship – friend, colleague, work,
home, school, Internet. There are all manner of relationships that
humans have in a lifetime, with people and with things. Social networks
present a layered relationship. They create and/or develop relationships
between people within a higher level relationship with a thing. This
'thing' is potentially alien to us – we use it not quite understanding all of
its rules. To quote Seinfeld, it is 'a backwards bizarro world'.[3] There are
people on the network who are known to the user, and digital traces of
everyday events, but due to the structure of the network and the manner
in which communication takes place, relationships are slightly twisted.
The chapters in this book highlight the importance of academic work,
such as Simmel's, regarding how everyday aspects of life affect human
relationships. I have also emphasised Benjamin's reference to a user as a
'screen actor'; a perspective through which their position is moderated.
It is the existence of the screen that allows a user the freedom to
communicate, but it also mediates the communication. This creates a
disconnection between the information that is being disclosed and the
results that it has on other users.

In this book I have tracked the life cycle of the digital presence. This discussion commenced by looking at what constitutes a digital presence and the information that needs to be disclosed in order to join a social network. A user is born into a social network through the creation of their digital presence. A digital presence is composed of a user's identity – biographical or 'About Me' information – and the actions of the digital presence – profile building, communicating and sharing information. Elaborating on technical and social aspects of different social networks such as gaming and online dating demonstrated how the reality of the user's life influences their digital presence.

The topic of celebrity is important to discussions of social networks, not only because they encourage users to participate and engage with them in networks such as *twitter*, but also because their distinct visibility highlights the different ways that the digital presence affects all users. In terms of celebrities and net-celebrities, social networks help a celebrity to build a digital presence, which in turn helps to create and solidify a fan base and popularity. Having a digital presence, however, can also have negative affects on a celebrity's life such as regarding privacy issues. I showed that celebrities' everyday comments, posted within social networks, are used without a context in entertainment stories. This shows that there is a lack of context and history that surrounds the everyday use of common network functions such as status updates. This highlights the presence and effects of everyday undercurrents within social networks.

Subsequently, different functions of social networks and how these functions promoted leisure activities, socialising and communication were discussed. Friends, photographs, videos, status updates and commenting were discussed in Chapter four to reveal how uploading this material adds to a digital presence, creates and develops friendships, provides a user with a social circle, and fosters communication. Friendship is an important element of this debate because, although being informed by some element of offline etiquette, how it operates in an online network differs. I have demonstrated the two-way flow of information between a digital presence and other aspects of the user's life and illustrated that there are several positive aspects to social networking. I have focused particularly on how the digital presence allows a user to create and maintain friendships or extend their social circle. The creation of micro-communities can have the important and positive affect of reducing feelings of isolation and providing a user with social 'worth'. In this respect networks can work to give a 'life' of sorts to those who otherwise may not have one.

Social networks, however, are a particularly powerful tool, and as networks of friends extend and more of a user's life is displayed through their own digital presence (and via other user's profiles) the two-way flow of information between a user's digital presence and other aspects of their life becomes more apparent. Given the amount of time that people spend in the workplace, the changing shapes of workplaces and the blurring of boundaries between work and leisure, the presence of social networks in the workplace is particularly relevant. Through a discussion of Web 1.0, the New Economy, the popular cultural workplace and Web 2.0 I explored not only the changing aesthetics and expectations of workplaces, but also the starring role that digital technologies play. I paid particular attention to the existence, expectation and (mis)use of social networks in workplaces. This revealed the insidious and problematic nature of social networks and how they infiltrate multiple facets of a user's life. Network elements such as photographs and status updates become destructive entities, whose misuse can result in the loss of respect, friendships and employment. These are the everyday undercurrents that negatively affect a user's life (as demonstrated with celebrities and status updates that were taken out of context). I have argued that users need to monitor their digital presence, which to some extent all users already do, but in deleting information from a profile, the context for content such as photographs and status updates can also be removed. This marks a descent into the negativity that exist in social networks. Digital technology is evolving at a rapid rate, as demonstrated by gaming in Chapter two. As it advances, different aspects of a user's life are drawn together. Work is such an intrinsic part of life and the ramifications of participation in social networks, both at and outside of work, demonstrates not only the two-way flow of information between a user and their digital presence, but also the negative ways that a digital presence can permeate everyday life.

Cyber-bullying, harassment, suicide and murder are all 'big' issues that have been linked to social networking websites. They have been highly publicised through news media and rightly so. The fact that the Internet and social networks seem to operate in a 'grey zone' and are considered by many to be faceless or a bubble, marks them as popular sites for misuse. I have looked at how these networks are used for cyber-bullying and harassment and the tragic consequences of doing so. Suicide and murder and their links to social networks were also discussed in order to illustrate the large, visible and tragic side of social network use. Shifting from the critical to the personal, I discussed everyday undercurrents affecting the user that mark networks as insidious and socially destructive forces. While creating, building and using a digital presence can be a positive experience, there are also constant negative consequences that go along with it. Much of this has to do with choice of friends, but it is really in the way that communication takes place – photographs, status updates, comments and chat – that is the real problem.

Throughout this book I have emphasised the two-way flow of information between user and digital presence. The main topics I have focused on are the flow of information that occurs through the varying communicative devices (primarily status updates), 'friendship' and evolving digital technology. All these elements are structured in a way to create a certain freedom in communication, a freedom that allows for many value-adding social experiences. Yet there is an apparent dissonance between technological literacy and a social literacy regarding the Internet and in particular social networks, which I believe involves the presence of a screen, as well as the structure of communication. There is an abundance of information that is without history or context that a user must make sense of. Through my own personal examples of social network use I demonstrated how the public and private everyday undercurrents of status updates, photographs and chat can leave the user in inappropriate social situations. Stepping away from the critical examination of social networks, these personal accounts allowed me to show that by choosing to have a digital presence and participate in social networks, you are choosing to be constantly bombarded with unwanted information. Users are faced with information and communication overload, which results in a clash between positive and negative networking experiences. Although we have the ability to monitor our digital presence (and so control the disclosure of our own information and some of our friends), being friends with someone means that we are limited in our ability to control the amount or types of information that we receive. Simply because we have the ability to communicate does not necessarily mean that it is good or that we should. Further research needs to be undertaken with regard to the psychological ramifications of channelling such a large proportion of information through social networks, but this does not fit into the scope of the present text. The final destination for this discussion is death.

Death, as previously discussed, is something often linked to social networks. A death offline, however, does not mean a death digitally. I discussed the immortalisation of a user's digital presence after they have died offline. I moved through the process of removing oneself from social networks, discussing various reasons for doing so – affliction, addiction and boredom. Death is the final stage in the journal of a digital presence, but removing information from a social network and the Internet altogether is not as easy as it was to be born. Digital traces and time limits on the suspension of information can make it difficult for an Internet user to remove the entirety of their digital presence.

Even if all of the information cannot be removed, attempting to remove a digital presence from social networks and the Internet is a cathartic process. Pulling in the reigns of those who have access to your life and gaining control of the information that you receive, provides a greater freedom than gazing at pages of information about things you do not wish to know, written by people you do not necessarily care about. Liberation comes with limiting the amount and types of information that is communicated about oneself. There is something attractive about mystery. Although the Internet and social networks can play positive and necessary roles in everyday lives, a user needs to control their engagement with these systems rather than let them control the user. Even if a user never enters a social network, it is nevertheless likely that there are images of them on such sites; this is not something that can be controlled, but the use of online social networks does not have to dominate the ways in which we communicate.

A digital presence can give a user a social circle, providing access to friends, groups, celebrities and fans, but it lacks context and history. This is evident in all areas of use, from having an expansive account with so many friends that a user updates with generalised comments, to a part-time user who dips in and out reading small bits of other users' threads and missing the point or joke. Even those who monitor their presence intently and delete their history entirely, leaving a half-filled profile and only posting sporadic cryptic updates are subject to this lack of context and history. This lacklustre approach to communication, encouraging profiles to be constantly filled with banal drivel, is definitely a source of leisure and perhaps social networks need to be treated as such. You would not play golf or go on holiday, to the beach, to the movies, to a nightclub or shopping and tell every person you meet about your life, showing them the pictures of your children or your Friday night out. As J. K. Rowling put it, 'it is our choices ... that show what we truly are'.[4] Social networks seem to give a freedom to communicate our lives to the world, to choose to follow people we admire or find interesting, or of whom we are remotely acquainted with. Yet this choice results in being overloaded with unnecessary and often offensive information. A user is left fighting the undercurrents of negativity and feelings of affliction. Finally, the realisation comes that choosing to communicate in this manner is not communicating effectively at all. The actions of a digital presence lack context, gesticulation, tone and feeling, and as a consequence, participation in a social network will always leave a user teetering on the edge of inappropriateness.

Notes

1. The Darkness (2005) 'Is it Just Me?' *One Way Ticket to Hell...and Back*. London: WEA/Atlantic.
2. Rammstedt, O. (1991) 'On Simmel's aesthetics: argumentation in the Journal *Jugend*, 1897–1906'. *Theory, Culture and Society*, 8(3): 126.
3. Ackerman, A. (dir.) (1996) 'Episode 137: The Bizarro Jerry', *Seinfeld*. New York: Castle Rock Entertainment.
4. Rowling, J. K. (1998) *Harry Potter and the Chamber of Secrets*. London: Bloomsbury, p. 245.

Index